30¢

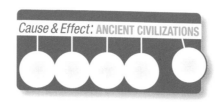

Cause & Effect: ANCIENT CIVILIZATIONS

Cause & Effect: Ancient India

Don Nardo

ReferencePoint Press®

San Diego, CA

About the Author

Historian and award-winning author Don Nardo has written numerous books about the ancient world, its peoples, and their cultures, including volumes on the Babylonians, Assyrians, Persians, Minoans, Greeks, Etruscans, Romans, Carthaginians, and others. In addition he is the author of single-volume encyclopedias on ancient Mesopotamia, ancient Greece, ancient Rome, and Greek and Roman mythology. Nardo, who also composes and arranges orchestral music, lives with his wife, Christine, in Massachusetts.

© 2018 ReferencePoint Press, Inc.
Printed in the United States

For more information, contact:
ReferencePoint Press, Inc.
PO Box 27779
San Diego, CA 92198
www. ReferencePointPress.com

LIBRARY OF CONGRESS CATALOGING-IN-PUBLICATION DATA

Name: Nardo, Don, 1947- author.
Title: Ancient India / by Don Nardo.
Description: San Diego, CA: ReferencePoint Press, Inc., 2018. | Series:
  Cause & effect: ancient civilizations | Includes bibliographical
  references and index.
Identifiers: LCCN 2016052619 (print) | LCCN 2016054834 (ebook) | ISBN
  9781682821541 (hardback) | ISBN 9781682821558 (eBook)
Subjects: LCSH: India—History—To 324 B.C. | India—History—324 B.C.–1000
  A.D. | India—Civilization.
Classification: LCC DS436 .N39 2018 (print) | LCC DS436 (ebook) | DDC
  934--dc23
LC record available at https://lccn.loc.gov/2016052619

CONTENTS

"History is a complex study of the many causes that have influenced happenings of the past and the complicated effects of those varied causes."

—William & Mary School of Education,
Center for Gifted Education

Understanding the causes and effects of historical events and time periods is rarely simple. The largest and most influential empire of ancient India, for instance, came into existence largely because of a series of events set in motion by Persian and Greek invaders. Although the Mauryan Empire was both wealthy and well organized and benefited enormously from strong rulers and administrators, the disarray sowed by invading forces created an opening for one of India's most ambitious and successful ancient rulers—Chandragupta, the man who later came to be known in the West as the "Indian Julius Caesar." Had conditions in India at the time been different, the outcome might have been something else altogether.

The value of analyzing cause and effect in the context of ancient civilizations, therefore, is not necessarily to identify a single cause for a singular event. The real value lies in gaining a greater understanding of that civilization as a whole and being able to recognize the many factors that gave shape and direction to its rise, its development, its fall, and its lasting importance. As outlined by the National Center for History in the Schools at the University of California–Los Angeles, these factors include "the importance of the individual in history . . . the influence of ideas, human interests, and beliefs; and . . . the role of chance, the accidental and the irrational."

ReferencePoint's Cause & Effect: Ancient Civilizations series examines some of the world's most interesting and important civilizations by focusing on various causes and consequences. For instance, in *Cause & Effect: Ancient India*, a chapter explores how one Indian ruler helped transform Buddhism into a world religion. And in *Cause & Effect: Ancient Egypt*, one chapter delves into the importance of the Nile River in the development of Egyptian civilization. Every book in the series includes thoughtful discussion of questions like these—supported by facts, examples, and a mix of fully documented primary and secondary source quotes. Each title also includes an overview of the civilization so that readers have a broad context for understanding the more detailed discussions of causes and their effects.

The value of such study is not limited to the classroom; it can also be applied to many areas of contemporary life. The ability to analyze and interpret history's causes and consequences is a form of critical thinking. Critical thinking is crucial in many professions, ranging from law enforcement to science. Critical thinking is also essential for developing an educated citizenry that fully understands the rights and obligations of living in a free society. The ability to sift through and analyze complex processes and events and identify their possible outcomes enables people in that society to make important decisions.

The Cause & Effect: Ancient Civilizations series has two primary goals. One is to help students think more critically about the human societies that once populated our world and develop a true understanding of their complexities. The other is to help build a foundation for those students to become fully participating members of the society in which they live.

IMPORTANT EVENTS IN THE HISTORY OF ANCIENT INDIA

ca. 2000 BCE
India's first advanced civilization, the Harappan, reaches its height of power in its urban, or city-oriented, culture.

ca. 1000 BCE
Vedic culture in India embarks on its final phase.

ca. 1900 BCE
The Harappans start abandoning most of their cities and revert back to a village-oriented society.

326 BCE
The Macedonian Greek conqueror Alexander (later called "the Great") invades India's Indus River valley and defeats the Indian raja Porus.

BCE 2000 / 1000 800 600 400

ca. 1500 BCE
Vedic culture begins to emerge in western India.

ca. 563 BCE
Prince Siddhartha Gautama is born; he later becomes known as the Buddha, or "Enlightened One."

ca. 424 BCE
Mahapadma Nanda comes to power in Magadha and increases the size and efficiency of the country's army.

ca. 543 BCE
Raja Bimbisara, who helps make the kingdom of Magadha the strongest nation-state in India, comes to power.

ca. 516 BCE
The Persians, led by King Darius I, invade western India.

ca. 200 BCE
Classical Hinduism begins to emerge in India.

323 BCE
Alexander dies unexpectedly in the Mesopotamian city of Babylon.

ca. 480 CE
A fierce Asian people—the Huns—invade India on their way to overrunning the Gupta Empire.

300 250 200 150 CE 300

ca. 322 BCE
Chandragupta Maurya founds a new dynasty in Magadha.

232 BCE
Ashoka, whose reign has been highlighted by his strong support for Buddhism, dies.

ca. 320 CE
A new ruling family, the Guptas, comes to power in Magadha and soon ushers in a so-called cultural and intellectual golden age.

335 CE
Samudragupta, son of the dynasty's founder, Chandragupta I, takes power.

ca. 260 BCE
The Mauryan ruler Ashoka severely defeats the kingdom of Kalinga.

India's Amazing Cultural Preservation

In 1856 Britain's East Indian Railway Company was in the midst of building a new line between the cities of Karachi and Lahore. (Both cities are now in Pakistan, which separated from India and became a new country in the 1940s.) Among the duties of two of the company's engineers—brothers John and William Brunton—was to find large quantities of track ballast (the materials forming the bed on which the railway ties rest).

One day John Brunton, who was working near Karachi, was fascinated to hear a local Indian tell him about an old abandoned city nearby. The place contained large amounts of bricks that would be perfect for ballast, the man said. "If all I had heard was true," Brunton later wrote, "this ruined city, built of bricks, would form a grand quarry for ballast."[1]

Brunton used those bricks for several miles of the railway bed. He also told his brother William, who was working farther north near Lahore, to be on the lookout for abandoned cities containing bricks. Sure enough, William soon found out about such a ruined city lying beside the modern village of Harappa, about 155 miles (250 km) from Lahore. Under his orders, the railway company plundered the ruins, removing hundreds of cartloads of bricks to use as ballast.

At the time, no one realized that Harappa had once been part of a large network of ancient cities spread across some 1.5 million square miles (3.9 million sq. km) of what was then western India. Those cities were part of a civilization—India's earliest advanced culture—dating from the 3000s and 2000s BCE. Modern archaeologists came to call that civilization Harappan, after the site of Harappa. It is also frequently referred to as the Indus Valley civilization, a reference to the Indus River, which flows through the region.

A Sameness over Centuries

Throughout the twentieth century and beyond, excavators who steadily uncovered some of the Harappan cities marveled at the sophistication of their builders. As in many modern cities, the streets were often laid in grid patterns. Also, the fired bricks used to construct the Harappan cities were water resistant, which made them perfect for erecting the drains found in most of the streets. "Such networks of drains," remarks archaeologist Charles Gates, "were a common and distinctive feature of Harappan cities. Such systems of public hygiene far surpassed contemporary Mesopotamian or Egyptian efforts."[2]

The orderly layout of streets, the use of fired bricks, and the installation and use of clever drainage systems were only some of the features found to be identical in all Harappan cities, no matter how distant from one another. Architectural styles were everywhere the same. Also, the residents of all the cities employed a unique, apparently universal writing script (which modern scholars have not yet deciphered). These facts led historians Bridget and Raymond Allchin to state, "Our overwhelming impression is of a sophisticated and highly complex society whose hallmark is—nevertheless—cultural uniformity, both throughout the several centuries during which the Harappan civilization flourished, and over the vast area it occupied."[3]

> "Our overwhelming impression is of a sophisticated and highly complex society."[3]
>
> —Historians Bridget and Raymond Allchin

This cultural sameness is all the more remarkable considering how long the Indus Valley civilization thrived. The results of the most recent studies of it were made public in 2016. They indicate that the Harappans erected their settlements, many of which eventually became urban centers (essentially, cities), over a period of more than three thousand years. Amazingly, numerous physical features of these centers remained little changed over all those centuries.

Preserving Culture

Even more astonishing is that this tendency to hold on to older cultural ideas and customs continued in later Indian societies and still exists in modern India. Indeed, a number of historians have remarked

A reconstruction shows what one of the Harappans' two largest cities, Mohenjo-daro, likely looked like in its heyday, in about 2600 BCE. The city's ruins now lie in Pakistan, which separated from India and became a new nation in 1947.

on how today's Indians are more in touch with their ancient past than the residents of other modern countries are with their own ancient pasts. A frequently cited example is Egypt. Its ancient inhabitants revered multiple gods, and many of their social customs were based on their beliefs associated with those deities. Yet Egypt was invaded and occupied by numerous outside peoples over the centuries, including Muslim Arabs and Turks. Most modern Egyptians, therefore, are now monotheistic Muslims with beliefs and customs far different from those of their ancient ancestors.

By contrast, a majority of modern Indians maintain numerous concepts and customs from a long series of ancient Indian cultures. Most Indians "still worship the same gods," one Indian scholar writes. Moreover, "they still chant the same verses and hymns which they recited 4,000 years ago."[4] Another historian, Alain Daniélou, makes the same point. He calls modern India "a sort of history museum, with its separate departments preserving the cultures, races, languages, and religions that have come into contact over its vast territory, without ever mixing together or destroying each other." Significantly, he adds, "no invader has ever entirely eliminated the cultures of the more ancient peoples, and new beliefs and knowledge have never supplanted the beliefs and knowledge of former times."[5]

> "[India is] a sort of history museum."[5]
>
> —Scholar Alain Daniélou

Some researchers have questioned whether this tendency toward cultural preservation began with the Harappans, who clearly maintained their cities, architectural styles, and language over long time periods. There is as yet no consensus among scholars as to whether this talent for cultural conservation passed on through the ages to modern India. If it did, it would be a potent example of historical cause and effect, the phenomenon in which one cultural idea or event leads directly to later ones.

More certain is that India has experienced a remarkable level of cultural preservation and continuity. It possesses a bewildering variety and complexity, historian Sinharaja Tammita-Delgoda explains. "Over the course of time it has come to accommodate many different peoples, each with its own customs and traditions, and all of them speaking their own languages. The result is a society with several different faces, composed of layer upon layer of varied social groups."[6]

CHAPTER ONE

A Brief History of Ancient India

N o one knows for sure when human beings first inhabited India's lush river valleys in the north; its large central plateau, called the Deccan, in the south; and its narrow, pleasant coastal plains in the southeast and southwest. The general scholarly consensus is that the first waves of outsiders arrived sometime between four hundred thousand and two hundred thousand years ago. They came from the west—the regions now occupied by Afghanistan and Iran.

Those earliest Indians had no permanent settlements. Rather, they were nomads—hunter-gatherers who followed migrating animal herds and foraged for roots, berries, and other plant foods. Archaeologists have unearthed no actual physical remains of the people in question. The evidence for their presence in India consists primarily of the stone tools they employed to slaughter the animals they killed to sustain themselves.

The first permanent settlements in the region coincided with the appearance of agriculture—between 7000 and 6000 BCE. The ability to grow food allowed the nomadic tribes to settle down in small villages. According to Sinharaja Tammita-Delgoda, the villagers "built houses of mud-brick, made their own pottery, and used stone and bone implements. They also bred their own livestock and raised sheep, goats, and cattle."[7] These tiny communities slowly grew in number and size, especially in the area around the Indus River valley, in western India (now part of Pakistan).

From Harappan to Vedic

It appears that a fair number of the valley's initial villages steadily grew into towns, each supporting more than one thousand people. In turn, some of the towns eventually became urban centers with populations of five thousand to thirty thousand or more. Spread out over most of western India, the inhabitants of this network of cities are now called the Harappans, after the ruined city near the modern village of Harappa.

Harappan culture, also known as the Indus Valley civilization, reached its height in the third millennium (2000s) BCE. In those centuries, the Harappans controlled an area twice the size of the lands ruled by the Egyptian pharaohs during the same era. It is tempting to assume that the Harappan cities and towns were part of a large-scale kingdom or empire. If that was true, it was Asia's first imperial realm. However, most modern experts think that the scattered Indus Valley communities were more likely independent city-states linked largely by their shared language and culture. The Harappans "resembled a loose federation of peoples rather than a unified state,"[8] remarks historian Gordon Johnson.

> "[The Harappans] resembled a loose federation of peoples rather than a unified state."[8]
>
> —Historian Gordon Johnson

Not much is known about Harappan culture. This is partly because the language its people spoke has not yet been deciphered. Also, beginning in about 1900 BCE, its cities steadily fell into disrepair, and over time all of them were eventually abandoned. In the many centuries that followed, later residents of the region stripped the ruins of most artifacts. Even many of the bricks of which the buildings were composed were carted away to be used in newer structures. All of that ancient plunder left little of a substantial nature about Harappan culture for modern archaeology to study and analyze.

One aspect of the Indus Valley civilization that twentieth-century historians found particularly difficult to understand was how it declined and seemingly disappeared. With so little substantial evidence to work with, many scholars assumed that members of the next successful culture in the region had invaded and wiped out the Harappans. Experts call that new civilization Vedic, after the Vedas, a collection of sacred verses revered and perpetuated by the area's new residents. The Vedas were composed in Sanskrit, a language that entered India from what is now Iran in the mid- to late second millennium BCE. The fact that Sanskrit came from Iran led many scholars to conclude that the Vedic people originated there, too, before invading India.

In this painting of a typical ancient Harappan street scene, people go about their daily routines, including fetching water from a well and making flour from wheat.

But most historians now think the Vedic people were, more or less, direct descendants of the Harappans. The current consensus is that major climatic changes and a shift in the kinds of crops grown, along with other factors not yet well understood, induced the Harappans to gradually abandon their urban culture. They returned to a village-centered existence. Over time, they also welcomed and absorbed immigrants from the west who spoke new languages and brought new ideas. All of these changes slowly but surely transformed at least some of the Harappans into the Vedic people.

Emergence of the Great Kingdoms

In whatever manner the Vedic culture emerged in western India, between 1500 and 1000 BCE its people steadily spread eastward into the Ganges River valley, as well as southward into central India. At first they were primarily rural herders who raised sheep and cattle. To supplement this emphasis on producing livestock—a system called pastoralism—they also grew a few crops.

The Vedic villages were initially small and impermanent. But during the last phase of Vedic culture—from about 1000 to 500 BCE—some of these settlements grew larger and became towns, and a few of the towns expanded into small cities. Another thing that changed during this period of gradual urbanization was the mainstay of the local economy. Cattle herding and other examples of pastoralism steadily gave way to larger-scale farming. Religious activities were also important, and a priestly class called the Brahmins emerged to lead common folk in worship.

No less important were political changes among the various Vedic tribes and cities. Several of the stronger independent cities absorbed their weaker neighbors and became fairly extensive kingdoms, each ruled by a local monarch called a raja. By around 600 BCE all of northern India, plus some portions of the south, had come to be divided into sixteen major realms of this sort. Modern scholars collectively call them the *Mahajanapadas*, meaning "Great Kingdoms" or "Great Countries." In the same period, an array of less-powerful kingdoms emerged farther west in the Indus River valley.

Most prominent among the sixteen Great Kingdoms was Magadha in northeastern India, a state destined to play a major role in later ancient Indian history. It became the richest and militarily the strongest of the Mahajanapadas, and by the early 540s BCE it dominated most of the Ganges River valley. Magadha's rajas carried on an ambitious policy of expansion. In the late 500s BCE, for example, one of them, King Bimbisara (reigned ca. 543–491 BCE), overran the kingdom of Kashi, located northwest of Magadha. Other neighboring realms the Magadhans conquered in the years that followed were Anga, on the northern rim of the Bay of Bengal, and Kosala, lying northwest of Kashi.

Foreigners Attack India

While Magadha and the other so-called Great Kingdoms were fighting for dominance in eastern India, some of the smaller realms in the Indus Valley faced the onslaught of some vigorous foreign invaders. The first of those intruders were the Persians. The Persian realm had fairly suddenly risen to prominence in Iran in the mid-500s BCE. While carving out the largest empire the world had yet seen, the first Persian king, Cyrus II, attacked and annexed Bactria (the ancient name for what is now northern Afghanistan). This placed the Persian Empire's eastern border alongside India's Indus Valley.

Not satisfied with staying on his own side of that border, Persia's third king—Darius I—invaded western India in about 516 BCE. Historians know very little about the incursion because surviving ancient accounts that mention it are sketchy at best. The fifth-century-BCE Greek historian Herodotus, for instance, said only that "Darius subdued the Indians" and thereafter "made regular use of the southern ocean,"[9] that is, the sea called the Indian Ocean today. Thus, it is unclear how much of western India the Persians came to control. Most modern experts think they never penetrated any Indian territory lying east of the Indus. So the peoples of Magadha and the other Great Kingdoms likely experienced the invasion only through secondhand verbal accounts.

The Persians introduced an undetermined number of linguistic, religious, and political ideas into western India. But these concepts proved relatively short lived because they were soon surpassed by a veritable tidal wave of influences from another foreign people—the Greeks. In 334 BCE, the Macedonian-Greek king Alexander III, later dubbed Alexander the Great, invaded the Persian-controlled Middle East and swiftly brought most of the Persian realm to its knees. By 327 BCE he had reached Bactria and the following year marched into the Indus Valley.

The Sixteen Mahajanapadas

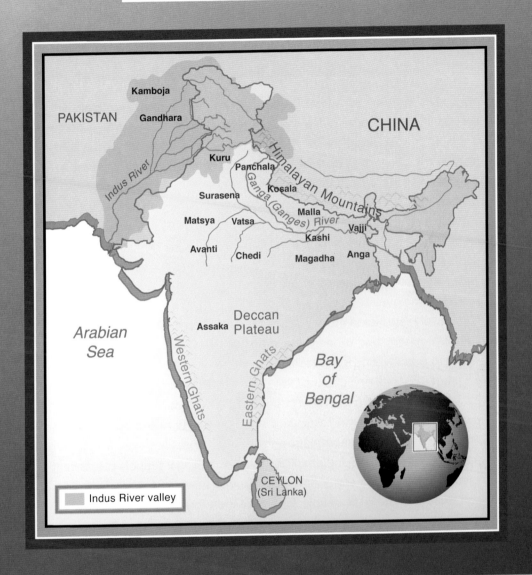

Many rulers in the region had heard about Alexander's military prowess, so they welcomed him rather than risk obliteration. One local Indian raja bravely decided to resist the invaders, however—Porus, of the kingdom of Pauravaa. That realm lay just east of the Hydaspes River. (*Hydaspes* is the Greek name for a major tributary of the Indus. Ancient Indians called it the Vitasta, and today it is known

Proof for Modern Indians' Harappan Ancestry

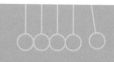

Most scholars now think that the Harappans were among the direct ancestors of most modern Indians. During much of the twentieth century, a majority of experts thought the opposite. They believed that the Vedic people, the direct ancestors of a majority of modern Indians, invaded India and overran the Harappans. However, more recent forensic and genetic studies, including DNA tests, have proved that scenario to be in error. In 1984 and again in 1991, some three hundred Harappan skeletons were examined closely. Experts also looked at the remains of some ancient Vedic people. The scientists who conducted the tests found no significant differences between the physical traits of the Harappan and Vedic individuals studied. Moreover, the tests showed that overall the Harappan skeletons very closely resembled those of most modern Indians. DNA samples of ancient Harappans and modern Indians were also conducted in the 1990s. The testers knew that, if the Vedic folk were actually a separate people who originated outside of India, the DNA of the Harappans and modern Indians (who descended from the Vedic people) should be noticeably different. Yet the results of these DNA tests were similar to those of the skeletal tests. There were no significant genetic or racial differences between the Harappans and most modern Indians. These studies strongly support the current theory—that at least some of the Harappans slowly but surely morphed, culturally, into the Vedic people, who were therefore *not* outsiders.

by its Muslim name, the Jhelum.) Porus was no military lightweight. His army numbered more than thirty thousand soldiers and some two hundred war elephants.

The great battle that took place beside the river in the spring of 326 BCE was hard fought by both sides, but Alexander prevailed. Afterward, Porus, who suffered wounds in the fierce combat, met with the victor. Alexander's chief ancient biographer, the Greek Arrian, reported that Alexander asked his opponent how he wished to be treated. The proud Porus answered, "As a king!"[10] Alexander was so impressed with

Porus's valor and noble bearing that he restored him to his throne. The condition was that the raja must now be a Greek ally and supply Alexander with food, weapons, and other supplies as needed.

The Mauryan Conquerors

Alexander intended to use such supplies when conquering the rest of India. He was especially intent on capturing Magadha, which he had heard was fabulously wealthy. But for various reasons his westward march halted, and then he died unexpectedly in 323 BCE at the age of only thirty-two. The impact of his conquest remained, however. Some of his Greek successors retained control of Bactria and parts of western India, where Greek cultural influences turned out to be substantial and long lasting.

Meanwhile, one powerful Indian state decided to take full advantage of Alexander's untimely death. Only two years after that key event, a new dynasty (family line of rulers)—the Mauryan—arose in Magadha. Its first raja, Chandragupta Maurya, saw Alexander's demise as an opportunity and led large-scale military expeditions toward the west. By about 311 BCE, he had captured all the lands stretching from Magadha westward to the Indus River, including a few of the areas Alexander had conquered less than two decades before.

Chandragupta turned out to be one of the most successful of all ancient rulers. The fourth-century-BCE Greek writer Megasthenes, who spent some time in the Mauryan court, called him a tireless, incredibly dedicated leader. "He remains in court for the whole day," Megasthenes wrote, "without allowing the business to be interrupted, even though the hour arrives when he must needs attend to his person."[11] Chandragupta was as ambitious as he was tireless, and he eventually seized control of nearly all of northern India. Later Western writers came to call him the "Indian Julius Caesar" (in reference to the famous Roman conqueror).

Chandragupta's son and successor, Bindusara, further expanded the Mauryan Empire, bringing large portions of the Deccan into the fold. Then Bindusara's own son, Ashoka, took the throne. Undoubtedly one of history's most extraordinary rulers, Ashoka was at first an ardent conqueror, as his father and grandfather had been. In about 260 BCE he attacked Kalinga, the only major Indian kingdom not yet under Mauryan control.

This painting shows Alexander's fearsome Macedonian phalanx in action. The pikemen bear down on the elephant corps of Indian ruler King Porus's army in the 326 BCE battle of Hydaspes.

After killing thousands of Kalingans, however, Ashoka had a sudden change of heart and went so far as to denounce the act of making war. The death and destruction caused by war "pains me,"[12] he told his people. He also converted to Buddhism, which preaches treating all living things with kindness.

Rise of the Guptas

Thereafter, Ashoka showed himself to be a fair and highly effective ruler. But most of the later Mauryan rajas who followed his death in 232 BCE displayed considerably less humanity and leadership skills. As a result, the realm steadily shrank in size, and many of its outlying provinces broke away and declared their independence. The last Mauryan ruler, Brihadratha, was assassinated in 184 BCE.

The long Mauryan rule over Magadha did leave behind a formidable legacy, however. The dynasty had forged the first political unit that encompassed almost all of India, a feat not repeated until modern times. As historian John Keay points out, "The ideal of a pan-Indian empire was never forgotten,"[13] and it motivated numerous later Indian rulers.

Nevertheless, when the last Mauryan raja died in 184 BCE, India was more fragmented and disunited than it had been in a long time. A number of less-than-memorable dynasties and rulers now rose and fell in the kingdoms that had broken away from Mauryan Magadha. Today's historians often call those states, which were modestly successful at best, the early "Middle Kingdoms."

It was not until the 320s CE that the greatest of the Middle Kingdoms, the Gupta realm, arose. Its ruling family, the Guptas, came to power in Magadha under circumstances that remain unclear. More certain is that the dynasty's founder, Chandragupta I (not to be confused with the Mauryan ruler of that name), united large portions of northern India. His son, Samudragupta (reigned 335–375 CE), continued that policy. When the latter passed away, the empire was almost as large as the one the Mauryan rulers had created.

> "The ideal of a pan-Indian empire was never forgotten."[13]
>
> —Historian John Keay

The Golden Age

In addition to his accomplishments as a politician and military leader, Samudragupta made a name for himself in cultural affairs. A musician and poet, he came to be called "the poet king" and sank a great deal of money into support for the arts. These efforts foreshadowed the emergence of a full-fledged cultural golden age under Samudragupta's successor, Chandragupta II (reigned 375–415).

That second of the dynasty's Chandraguptas assumed the title Vikramaditya, meaning "he whose splendor equals the sun." He was a successful imperialist who by the year 409 had brought all of western India under Gupta control. He also expanded the economy, significantly raising the overall level of prosperity. A Chinese traveler, Fa-Hsien, who visited India between 405 and 411 said of Magadha's heartland, "The cities and towns of this country are the greatest of all

The Indian Shakespeare

The Gupta age witnessed the flourishing of a number of talented poets and other writers. The most successful was Khalidasa, a playwright and poet who in modern times came to be called the "Indian Shakespeare." Like the real Shakespeare, Khalidasa was able to present a wide range of human emotions in a universal manner that surpassed his own time and place and spoke to people in all later ages. In this passage from his work titled *The Birth of the War-God*, he captured a gesture of kindness overcoming deep pain and anguish. After the sudden death of the god Love, his wife, Charm, is overcome by sorrow. But Love's male friend, the deity Spring, comforts her and prevents her from dying of grief.

> [Spring said] "So, gentle Charm, preserve your body sweet
>   For dear reunion after present pain;
> The stream that dwindles in the summer heat,
>   Is reunited with the autumn rain."
>
> Invisibly and thus mysteriously
>   The thoughts of Charm were turned away from death;
> And Spring, believing where he might not see,
>   Comforted her with words of sweetest breath.
>
> The wife of Love awaited thus the day,
>   Though racked by grief, when fate should show its power,
> As the waning moon laments her darkened ray
>   And waits impatient for the twilight hour.

Khalidasa, *The Birth of the War-God*, trans. Arthur W. Ryder, Internet Sacred Text Archive. www.sacred-texts.com.

[the ones] in [India]. The inhabitants are rich and prosperous, and vie with one another in the practice of benevolence and righteousness."[14]

Although not all Indians under the Guptas were actually wealthy, the government created a sort of welfare system that provided the poor, disabled, and others in need with a safety net. According to Fa-Hsien, the cities featured "houses for dispensing charity and medicines. All the poor and destitute in the country, orphans, widowers, and childless men, maimed people, and cripples, and all who are diseased, go to those houses, and are provided with every kind of help, and doctors examine their diseases. They get the food and medicines which their cases require, and are made to feel at ease."[15]

> "The inhabitants are rich and prosperous, and vie with one another in the practice of benevolence."[14]
>
> —Ancient Chinese traveler Fa-Hsien

Medical advances were only one aspect of a veritable golden age of the arts and sciences under Vikramaditiya. Mathematics thrived as Indian scholars devised the decimal system and the concept of zero, concepts that later passed to Europe via the Arabs. Also, Gupta astronomers calculated the length of the solar year and determined that the earth is a sphere rather than a flat disk. In literature, meanwhile, many talented writers plied their craft. Perhaps the finest was Khalidasa, a playwright and poet who centuries later came to be compared in quality to England's great William Shakespeare.

Rapid Decline

India's cultural golden age turned out to be much shorter than Vikramaditiya had hoped it would be. Following his death in 415, the Gupta realm declined rapidly. The worst blows to stability and prosperity were two invasions by the Huns—a ferocious and brutal Asian people—in the late 400s. After India had suffered much death and destruction, a shaky alliance of rajas just barely managed to overcome the intruders in the sixth century. But by that time, most of India had shattered into numerous small, weak, and disunited states. Modern experts see that period as the end of India's ancient age and start of its long medieval era.

CHAPTER TWO

What Part Did India's Early Cultures Play in the Birth of Hinduism?

Focus Questions

1. Why do you think some ancient religions have died out while others have endured—and thrived—for hundreds or even thousands of years?
2. What are the primary differences between polytheistic and monotheistic faiths? How is Hinduism both different from and similar to these belief systems?
3. How do the social structures of other civilizations in history compare with the caste system? What are the similarities, if any? What are the differences, if any?

Ancient India is sometimes compared to ancient Mesopotamia and ancient Egypt in the sense that they were all river cultures that acted as so-called cradles of human civilization. From this standpoint, they indeed had much in common. Each developed agriculture very early, erected cities with populations in the thousands, and developed the world's earliest empires.

One point on which these early civilizations markedly differed was their contribution, or lack thereof, to the creation of universal world religions. The Sumerians and Babylonians in ancient Mesopotamia and the ancient Egyptians were devoutly religious. However, for the most part their faiths disappeared after their civilizations declined. Only a tiny handful of modern people show an interest in following the precepts of those mostly extinct religions.

By contrast, ancient India gave rise to no less than three faiths that over the course of time grew into great world religions that still have millions of adherents. Those major religions are Hinduism, Buddhism, and Jainism. Of these, the Hindu faith both was the earliest to develop and has the most followers within modern India. Indeed, roughly 80 percent of modern India's more than 1 billion residents are Hindus.

Historians have determined that Hinduism developed directly from the beliefs and rituals of the Vedic culture, which emerged in the second millennium BCE. Moreover, mounting evidence indicates that Vedic beliefs developed at least in part from the religious ideas and customs of the earlier Harappans. Whatever the Harappan contributions may have been, as Vedic worshippers added new gods and concepts over the course of centuries, the Vedic religion evolved little by little. Finally, evidence shows, it attained its most mature and complex version in Hinduism.

The Central Hindu Beliefs

That more mature form of Hinduism, which with a few minor differences is still practiced today, is often called classical Hinduism. Although Hindus worship multiple gods, the religion does not have the traditional characteristics of other polytheistic faiths, particularly belief in multiple gods who are completely separate beings. Hinduism actually combines certain facets of monotheism with polytheism. One of the central beliefs of classical Hinduism, for instance, is that there exists a universal spirit, which Hindus call the *ishvara*. Most Hindus see the *ishvara* as a "one true god" named Brahma. According to Hindu beliefs, that universal divine being is able to take on diverse alternate personalities, at times simultaneously, and among those disguises are the other Hindu gods. Perhaps the best known among those other deities are Vishnu, the universe's preserver and protector; Shiva, the so-called destroyer, who brings large-scale change, often beneficial; Indra, deity of rain and storms; and Lakshmi, goddess of wealth and purity.

In a similar manner, Hinduism professes that each of these gods— still a part of the single, universal god Brahma—can manifest itself, or appear, in alternative forms. A good example is Vishnu. In Hindu literature, he assumes several earthly disguises, frequently called avatars, or incarnations, including the hero Rama and the hero-prankster-lover Krishna. The Hindus also recognize some angel-like beings—the *devas*—and several evil demons—the *asuras*.

An engraving depicts the Hindu creator deity Brahma. Showing him with multiple faces captured the idea that Hindus envision him as the sole existing god and that other perceived divine beings are various sides of his personality.

In addition, Hinduism embraces the idea of reincarnation, seen as the continued rebirth of the human soul (the *atman*). It is thought that such a soul is eternal and moves into another body at the moment of death. According to an ancient Indian text, the Bhagavad Gita, "As a man discards worn-out clothes to put on new and different ones, so the embodied self discards its worn-out bodies to take on other new ones."[16] Supposedly, this mystical progression continues as the soul attempts to steadily improve in hopes of eventually achieving oneness, or union, with the universal spirit—Brahma.

Strongly affecting this process, Hindus believe, is karma, a pitiless law of moral consequences. "Karma governed the relationship between one's actions in one incarnation and one's station in the next," writes Sinharaja Tammita-Delgoda. "Merit was rewarded, but sin had to be atoned for. Thus, the merit and the sins of the past life were visited on the next. According to karma, we are what we are because of what we were and what we did."[17]

> "According to karma, we are what we are because of what we were and what we did."[17]
>
> —Historian Sinharaja Tammita-Delgoda

Finally, early Hindus adopted a social structure that ranks people by their so-called importance in society, as well as by the occupations that are considered proper for them to take. That structure primarily consists of four main castes, or groupings that resemble social classes. The highest caste is made up of religious teachers and academic scholars; next come public servants, including leaders and keepers of law and order; then those involved in business and other commercial activities; and fourth, skilled and unskilled laborers. For a long time, beneath the four main castes was a fifth—the "untouchables," seen as inferior social outcasts. (Discrimination against the untouchables was outlawed in India's constitution in the twentieth century but still lingers in some quarters of the country.)

Evidence from Harappan Seals and Figurines

To answer the question of how India's earliest cultures—the Harappan and Vedic—gave birth to a religion that evolved into classical Hinduism, one must begin long ago among the Harappan cities in the Indus Valley. When historians first tried to tackle this question, they immediately ran into some serious difficulties. This was partly because the Harappans' language was not yet decoded—and it remains mostly undeciphered today. As a result, there was no way to tell if that tongue's surviving texts contained descriptions of gods and religious rituals and/or sacred hymns to such deities.

Harappan Concepts in Hinduism?

A number of modern experts support the idea that Harappan culture and its religion likely contributed at least some fundamental concepts and deities to what would later become Hinduism. They base that supposition in part on the evidence of images on surviving Harappan seals. Some of those objects contain fairly routine, nonreligious themes or concepts. But others show images suggestive of later Vedic and proto-Hindu religious ideas and symbols. One often-cited example is the Pashupati seal. Discovered in 1928 in the Harappan city of Mohenjo-daro, it has been roughly dated to the period between 2350 and 2000 BCE. The seal shows a horned god, who appears to be meditating, surrounded by five animals—a tiger, deer, elephant, buffalo, and rhinoceros. Experts point out that those creatures likely represented the five primary elements/forces recognized in most ancient societies—earth, water, fire, wind, and air (or empty space). Later Vedic religion and literature recognize those same substances as the Five Great Elements. Moreover, says Indian scholar N.S. Rajaram, "Hindu cosmology [concepts relating to the universe's creation] holds that both creation and destruction of the universe result from the action of the Five Great Elements." The Pashupati seal and other similar Harappan seals therefore seem to imply that at least a few Harappan religious concepts passed on to the Vedic faith and from there to classical Hinduism.

N.S. Rajaram, "Beyond Decipherment: The Message of the Indus Seals," Archaeology Online. archaeologyonline.net.

Nevertheless, formal writings are not the only Harappan evidence that archaeologists and other scholars have had the good fortune to examine. That ancient people also left behind some physical, artistic evidence in the form of drawings (most often on pottery) and figurines and other sculptures. There are also carvings on seals—small objects, usually made of stone, used to make impressions in soft clay (which dried to form baked clay tablets). Those marks were made by society's rich and famous, along with merchants, to stamp their authority on such permanent records.

Of the hundreds of Harappan seals uncovered so far, the images on several suggest the existence of concepts and customs not unlike some of those in the Hindu faith. The swastika, for instance, had a number of meanings in early Hinduism, including the bestowing of blessings or good luck on someone. This symbol, which the Nazis adopted as their emblem in the 1930s, has been seen in some of the seals excavated in the Indus Valley. As St. John's College scholar Peter Britton says, this is only one of several "intriguing indications of continuity between the religion"[18] of the Harappans and both the Vedic faith and early Hinduism.

Numerous Harappan seals also "show animals presented in a format reminiscent of later Hindu gods such as Shiva and Indra," Britton continues. In addition, he points out the suggestive evidence in surviving carved figurines: "The large number of figurines found in the Indus Valley have led some scholars to argue that the Indus people worshipped a mother goddess symbolizing fertility, a common practice among rural Hindus even today. All these pieces of evidence point to the Indus Valley religion having a large measure of influence on the beliefs and practices of the Vedic people who came after them."[19]

> "The large number of figurines found in the Indus Valley have led some scholars to argue that the Indus people worshipped a mother goddess symbolizing fertility."[19]
>
> —Scholar Peter Britton

The Vedic Religious Texts

Although links between the Harappan religion and classical Hinduism are still somewhat uncertain and debated by scholars, no doubts exist among experts that the Vedic people's faith was the direct ancestor of later Hinduism. One reason they are sure is that, unlike the Harappan script, the Vedic language—Sanskrit—is well understood. Moreover, several long, detailed Vedic literary texts have survived intact, and they reveal many of the Vedic people's religious beliefs and myths. Those works also describe some of the main Vedic social and political customs. Of the texts in question, the best known are the Vedas. Researcher Cristian Violatti explains:

We do not know much about the authors of these texts. In Vedic tradition the focus tends to be on the ideas rather than on the authors, which may allow one to look at the message without being influenced by the messenger. Vedic literature is religious in nature and as such tends to reflect the worldview, spiritual preoccupations, and social attitudes of the Brahmans or priestly class of ancient India.[20]

The oldest of the Vedas is the Rig-Veda (meaning "Rich in Knowledge"). It is divided into ten books, each featuring a number of hymns to various Vedic gods. Three other Vedas—the Sama-Veda, Yajur-Veda, and Atharva-Veda—were written somewhat later than the Rig-Veda. Not long after 1000 BCE, some Brahmins introduced some Vedic texts seemingly designed to explain and/or comment on the original Vedas. These supplementary works include the Brahminas and Upanishads.

Vedic writers also composed ancient India's two huge and magnificent epic poems—the *Ramayana* and the *Mahabharata*. The *Ramayana* recounts the exploits of a heroic prince, Rama, who was also said to be an incarnation, or living form, of the god Vishnu (who in classical Hinduism is himself a manifestation of the universal spirit Brahma). The *Mahabharata* describes a complex, exciting struggle for a royal kingly throne, events overseen by divine beings who hold humanity's fate in their mighty hands.

> "In Vedic tradition the focus tends to be on the ideas rather than on the authors, which may allow one to look at the message without being influenced by the messenger."[20]
>
> —Researcher Cristian Violatti

For a long time these Vedic texts—which later became sacred to Hinduism—were perpetuated orally. Priests and/or some special non-priestly performers memorized and recited them in public during religious festivals. The two epics were not committed to writing until around 500 to 400 BCE, and it appears that the first written versions of the Vedas themselves did not emerge until later, possibly as late as 300 BCE.

Vedic Social Classes, Gods, and Rituals

The various Vedic writings show that India's ancient Vedic society came to be divided into four broad social classes, the *varnas*. This was

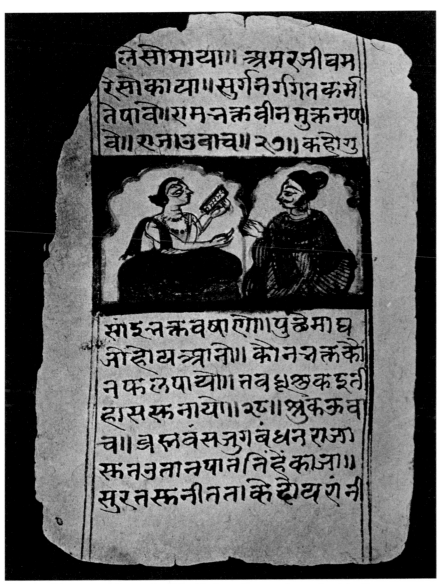

Pictured is a page from the Rig-Veda, a key early ancient Indian document most likely composed sometime between 1500 and 1200 BCE. It contains 1,028 hymns dedicated to various gods held sacred by the ancient Vedic people.

clearly the precursor of the social structure that became the traditional caste system among India's later Hindus. The smallest and most respected varna was that of the priests—the Brahmins, who were in charge of overseeing and interpreting the holy Vedic texts.

In order of descending importance in the Vedic social breakdown, the second varna was the warrior class—known as the Kshatriyas. It included the kings (rajas), their leading advisers and military officers, and other well-to-do and influential people. The third varna, called the Vaishyas, was composed of traders, merchants, artisans, and other reputable workers. The last and lowest varna, which also made up the bulk of the population, was the Sudras. Its members were everyday laborers who usually served those of the upper classes.

The four varnas derived from descriptions of social groups found in the Rig-Veda. But the concept of the fifth class—or more accurately, *under*class—the untouchables, did not emerge until the 300s CE or somewhat later. What made these folk "untouchable" was that they usually did jobs seen to be polluting, or ritually unclean, to society as a whole. Such supposedly demeaning tasks included handling corpses, especially burning them on communal pyres, and physically carrying out executions. (These jobs are still seen as filthy and undignified by many modern Indians.)

A painting shows the ancient god Indra, leader of the Vedic deities. Worshippers anoint, or rub, him with soma, juice from an unidentified plant that was widely employed in Vedic and early Hindu religious rituals.

In a similar manner, many of the Vedic gods and the beliefs and rituals surrounding them were later incorporated into the more mature form known as classical Hinduism. The principal Vedic deity, Indra, is a well-known example. Initially, he was the chief war deity, as well as the controller of the weather. Classical Hinduism kept him in its pantheon (overall group of gods) but reduced his importance. Other important Vedic gods who later found their places in Hinduism's divine assembly were Agni, deity of fire and knowledge; Soma, the moon god; Surya, the god of the sun; Vayu, the deity of the winds; Varuna, lord of water and the oceans; and Mitra, god of truth.

A great many of the Vedic gods were divine manifestations of natural forces such as storms, fire, and wind. The Rig-Veda mentions these various beings in a large number of hymns. But three principal deities get more attention than most. "More than half the hymns," Violatti says "invoke just three top-rated gods of the moment: Indra (250 hymns), Agni (200 hymns), and Soma (just over 100 hymns)." Of the first of these deities, he goes on,

> the Vedas describe Indra as the god "who wields the thunderbolt," and his most celebrated story was the killing of the demon-serpent Vritra. The legend says that Vritra kept all the waters trapped in his mountain lair, and Indra was the one who slew the demon in order to release the waters. Soma was the personification [essence] of the sacred soma plant, whose juice was holy and intoxicating to gods and men. Agni, the god of fire, is often referred to in Vedic literature as the most important god, and is considered to be the flame that lifts the sacrifice to heaven, a symbol of the fiery life and spirit of the world.[21]

Worship of Indra, Agni, and the other original Vedic gods did not take place in temples, sacred structures introduced in later centuries in India. Rather, Vedic worshippers gathered around hearth-like outdoor altars to witness fire sacrifices, the leading religious ritual of pre-classical Hindu India. Brahmin priests, thought to be divinely inspired by the fire god, Agni, lit supposedly sacred fires and led the worshippers in chanting hymns. The belief was that these rituals both pacified the gods and cleansed the worshippers of evil and impurities.

Early Classical Hindu Concepts

Just as aspects of Harappan religion seem to have transitioned into the Vedic faith, Vedic beliefs and rituals went on to evolve into classical Hinduism, which began to emerge in about 200 BCE. The Hindu faith retained Vedic rites such as fire ceremonies and hymn chanting. Yet the Hindus added some crucial new ideas and customs. One important addition was the creator god Brahma, whose image con-

Hymn to the Fire God

Among the original Vedic gods who were later absorbed into classical Hinduism was Agni, the fire deity. The second book of the Vedic text known as the Rig-Veda contains ten hymns to Agni, one of which includes these words of praise.

Among the tribes of men the Gods placed Agni as a dear friend when they would dwell among them. . . . Sweet is his growth as of one's own possessions. His look when rushing, willing to burn, is lovely. He darts his tongue forth, like a harnessed horse who shakes his flowing tail among the bushes. Since they who honor him have praised his greatness, he gave, as it was, his hue to those who love him. Known is he by his bright delightful splendor, and getting old renews his youth forever. Like one who is thirsty, he lights up the forests. Like water, down the chariot ways he roars. On his black path he shines in burning beauty, marked as it was the heaven that smiles through vapor.

Around, consuming the broad earth, he wanders free, roaming like an ox without a herdsman. Agni brightly shining, burning up the bushes, with blackened lines, as though the earth he seasoned. I, in remembrance of your ancient favor, have sung my hymn in this our third assembly. O Agni, give us wealth with store of heroes and mighty strength in food and noble offspring.

Rig-Veda, Book 2, Hymn no. 4, trans. Ralph T.H. Griffith, Internet Sacred Text Archive. www .sacred-texts.com.

tained a fresh, in certain ways revolutionary way of seeing the gods and the very concept of divinity. The older Vedic gods had been part of a traditional polytheistic belief system. In it, as in most other ancient polytheistic systems around the globe, worshippers revered a number of deities viewed as completely separate beings. By marked contrast, the emerging classical Hindus saw Brahma as a universal spirit similar in certain ways to the single god worshipped by Jews, Christians, and Muslims.

The classical Hindus also embraced the Vedic concept of reincarnation, as described in the Bhagavad Gita, as well as the idea of karma. Both reincarnation and karma buttressed and perpetuated the caste system in ancient Hindu India. Individuals' social status and moral worth were in theory often reflected in where their soul went following death. If people did disgraceful things in their lifetime, it was thought that karma would kick in and cause them to be punished. They might be reborn into a lower caste or even return as an animal.

No one knows for sure whether the Harappans knew the concept of karma. The Vedic people, who descended from the Harappans, were clearly familiar with that idea, although exactly when they first recognized it is unknown. More certain is that the Harappan/Vedic culture set the stage in various ways for the later development of Hinduism. As the late, noted historian Mortimer Wheeler put it, that long-lasting Indus Valley society exhibited some "specific manifestations of later Hinduism,"[22] including the creation of its basic written scriptures. Therefore, the Hindu faith, which remains India's chief religion today, emerged directly out of the religious ideas and beliefs of India's first advanced civilization.

CHAPTER THREE

How Did Alexander's Invasion of India Alter Indian Culture?

Focus Questions

1. Do you see the mixing of cultures as a positive or negative occurrence—and why? Provide examples to support your reasoning.
2. If you had been one of the leaders faced with the decision to welcome or resist Alexander and his army, which choice would you have made—and why? Can you think of any other options they could have pursued?
3. Which aspects of Greek culture made the most impact on the development of Indian civilization—and why?

Today when most people think of India, they picture a vast, populous, prosperous east Asian nation having little to do, culturally speaking, with the faraway European countries. Certainly, the small European nation of Greece might appear far removed from India in the areas of language, religion, science, and art. Yet the truth is actually the opposite. Deeply imbedded in modern Indian culture—subtle, well hidden, but very real—are multiple threads of ancient Greek thought, speech, and artistic styles.

These aspects of Indian culture came from an infusion of Greek culture that began with the now famous invasion of the Indus Valley by Alexander the Great in the 320s BCE. His personal presence in the region was short lived. After defeating the Indian raja Porus in 326 BCE, he returned to the Persian capital of Babylon, which he had recently captured. There, to the surprise of supporters and enemies alike, he died (possibly of alcohol poisoning) in 323 BCE.

Yet Greek influence on India did not die with Alexander. Some of his successors remained in the Indus Valley, and a few of them even penetrated more deeply into Indian territory. Moreover, in the decades that followed, Greek merchants, artisans, and settlers poured into western India. They and their children and grandchildren created a blended culture—often called either Greco-Indian or Indo-Greek—that subsequently had a measurable impact on developing Indian culture as a whole. Indian researcher Sanujit, who has written extensively on the Greeks in India, summarizes that impact, saying that it

> combined the Greek and Indian languages and symbols, as seen on [later Indian] coins, and blended ancient Greek, Hindu and Buddhist religious practices, as seen in the archaeological remains of [Indo-Greek] cities and in the indications of [local Greek] support of Buddhism. The Indo-Greek kings seem to have achieved a level of cultural syncretism [mixing] with no equivalent in history, the consequences of which are still felt today, particularly through the diffusion and influence of Greco-Buddhist art.[23]

Alexander Marches on India

Well before Alexander entered India, the rajas of all the region's kingdoms had heard detailed reports of his adventures in the Middle East. They were aware that he, a man only in his twenties, had managed to conquer Persia, the largest empire the world had yet seen, in short order. Many Indian leaders likely hoped that the ambitious Macedonian Greek king would steer clear of their lands.

But this was not to be. After seizing the various Persian capitals in what are now Iraq and Iran, Alexander marched his army eastward into Bactria. Soon it became clear that he meant to continue onward and push into the Indus Valley. "Like a tidal wave," John Keay writes, "news of Alexander's prowess had swept ahead of him,

"The consequences of [the Greek presence in ancient India] are still felt today, particularly through the diffusion and influence of Greco-Buddhist art."[23]

—Indian researcher Sanujit

The members of King Porus's elephant corps prepare to meet Alexander's army in battle on the banks of the Hydaspes River. During the encounter, several of the beasts panicked and crushed some of Porus's troops.

flattening resistance and sucking him forward."[24] The leaders of western India's nation-states now faced a very real dilemma. Should they try, as the Persians had, to resist the obviously formidable young Greek military phenom? Also, if the biggest empire on earth could not stand up to him, could they?

Most rajas in the region decided that the answer to both those questions was no. So several of them sent ambassadors to Alexander, offering him friendship and promising their support. (It is possible that some of them thought he might help them defeat Magadha, then India's military powerhouse, a feat they could not accomplish on their own.) To his delight, therefore, in the spring of 326 BCE Alexander crossed the Indus River and received a warm welcome in the city of Taxila (its Greek name—a garbled form of its Indian name, Takshachila). Taxila was the capital of a small Indian kingdom known as Hindus (or "Indus country").

Alexander was less happy to hear that Porus, raja of the neighboring kingdom of Pauravaa, was not ready to capitulate to the Greeks. This challenge could not be disregarded. In theory, Alexander could have simply ignored Porus, marched around Pauravaa, and moved deeper into India. But he knew that he could not allow Porus to defy him, because it would set a bad example for other Indian rulers who might try to resist. With this in mind, Alexander, now reinforced by five thousand Indian soldiers from Taxila, headed for a showdown with Porus along the Hydaspes River.

In the bloody battle that followed, Porus's troops were reinforced by many war elephants. But these beasts were not enough to stop the Greek onslaught. In fact, at one point some elephants panicked and fell back on and trampled Porus's men, causing numerous injuries. Although the Indian soldiers fought bravely, Alexander's battle-hardened forces and his own smart strategy won the day. The enormity of the Greek victory can be discerned in the casualty figures. According to Alexander's ancient biographer Arrian, "Nearly 20,000 of the Indian infantry were killed," along with "about 3,000 of their cavalry [mounted fighters]. All their war chariots were destroyed." In comparison, "Out of Alexander's original 6,000 infantry, some eighty were killed. In addition to these, he lost ten mounted archers,"[25] and about 220 of his cavalry.

> "Like a tidal wave, news of Alexander's prowess had swept ahead of him, flattening resistance and sucking him forward."[24]
>
> —Historian John Keay

Later Greeks in Bactria and India

Highly motivated by his victory, Alexander set his sights on moving eastward and attacking the kingdom of Magadha. He had been told by his Indian allies that that nation was the strongest in all of India. If he defeated it, they said, all the surrounding kingdoms would probably surrender without a fight. The problem was that Alexander was unable

Although modern historians are not absolutely certain, they think that the use of elephants in battle began in India during the late Vedic age, sometime between 1000 and 500 BCE. Thereafter, the practice spread outward to other lands, including Persia. It was there that Alexander and his soldiers first encountered the great beasts in combat. In the battle the Greeks fought with the Indian raja Porus along the banks of the Hydaspes River in 326 BCE, the Indians had hundreds of elephants. According to Alexander's ancient biographer, the Greek Arrian, Porus's use of these creatures ended up backfiring. As Alexander led his cavalry in a devastating charge against one group of Indian troops, Arrian wrote, those Indians

> fell back in confusion upon the elephants, their impregnable fortress, or so they hoped. The elephant drivers forced their beasts to meet the opposing cavalry, while the Greek infantry, in its turn, advanced against them, shooting down the drivers, and pouring in a hail of missiles from every side upon the elephants themselves. It was an odd bit of work—quite unlike any previous battle. The monster elephants plunged this way and that among the lines of infantry, dealing destruction.... [Soon] the elephants were boxed up, with no room to maneuver, by troops all around them, and as they blundered about, wheeling and shoving this way and that, they trampled to death as many of their friends as their enemies. [The Indian cavalry] suffered severely.

Arrian, *Anabasis Alexandri*, published as *The Campaigns of Alexander*, trans. Aubrey de Sélincourt. New York: Penguin, 1986, p. 278.

to keep his men from finding out how large and strong the Magadhan army was, not to mention the armies of other Indian states. According to another ancient biographer, Plutarch, the Greeks heard frightening rumors. On the far side of the Ganges River, there supposedly "swarmed a gigantic host of infantry, horsemen, and elephants. It was said that the kings of the [area] were waiting for Alexander's attack with an army of eighty thousand cavalry, two hundred thousand infantry, eight thousand chariots, and six thousand fighting elephants."[26]

These estimates were almost certainly hugely exaggerated. But Alexander's followers believed them. The soldiers were already worn out from years of hard combat far from home, and that fact, combined with their fear of the dangers that seemed to lurk ahead, filled them with despair. They told their commander, who they otherwise tremendously respected, that they simply would go no farther.

Greatly disappointed, Alexander returned to Babylon, where he died three years later. His leading generals and administrators almost immediately began fighting one another for control of the vast empire he had acquired. Hearing this, Magadhan leaders took advantage of the chaos among the Greeks and overran some of India's western territories Alexander had recently conquered.

Nevertheless, Bactria and some nearby stretches of western India stayed under Greek control, and Greek settlers continued to enter these lands. For a while, they were ruled by Seleucus, one of Alexander's chief successors, who also had charge of Iran and Iraq. In 250 BCE, however, the Greeks of Bactria broke free of Seleucus's realm and founded a nation of their own—the Greco-Bactrian Kingdom.

As time went on, moreover, the development of new Greek states in the area continued. In 180 BCE, for instance, the army of Demetrius, son of the Greco-Bactrian king Euthydemus I, marched well into western India. Indeed, in a mere five years Demetrius and his trusty military commander Menander seized the whole Indus Valley, along with a few territories lying beyond it. Then history repeated itself as Demetrius and Menander broke away from the Greco-Bactrian realm and set up their own country, the Indo-Greek Kingdom. Following Demetrius's death, Menander succeeded him and went on to become an unusually strong ruler. His successors on the Indo-Greek throne remained in power until 10 BCE, more than three centuries after Alexander had entered India.

Currency and Language

Thus, Greeks ruled parts or all of the Indus Valley for considerably longer than the United States has been a nation. During these centuries, many generations of Greeks knew only India as their home and introduced numerous Greek ideas to the region. Further, large numbers of them intermarried with locals. The overall result was the emergence of a hybrid Greco-Indian culture in which not only did Indians adopt Greek customs, but also many Greeks absorbed Indian customs. A good example is when Menander and large numbers of other Indo-Greeks converted to Buddhism. (That faith began in India before spreading to other lands.)

In a like manner, Greek coinage styles spread across India and remained in use for many centuries. Some ancient Indians began using coins about two centuries before Alexander's incursion into the re-

Some aspects of ancient Indian science had ripple effects that impacted people in the region well into modern times. For example, the creators of this 1840 image of Muslim astronomers were influenced by ancient Hindu charts showing planets and stars.

gion. They sometimes exchanged them for coins from foreign peoples they traded with. Coins from Persia and faraway Greece, plus some of the coins that Alexander minted, have been found in ancient ruins in western India.

The first Greek coins actually minted inside India were those of the Indo-Greek ruler Menander. The front of each shows his image and calls him "savior king" in Greek; the back displays that and other words in a local Indian language. Indeed, Sanujit explains, "most of the coins of the Greek kings in India were bilingual, written in Greek on the front and in Pali [an ancient Indian language] on the back." This was "a superb concession to another culture never before made in the Greek world." He adds, "The coinage of the Indo-Greeks remained in fact influential for several centuries throughout the Indian subcontinent."[27] Moreover, for centuries after the Indo-Greeks declined, numerous later Indian peoples and nations adopted Greek-style coins of their own.

Another significant Greek cultural influence felt throughout most of ancient India was in the area of language. Considering that hundreds of thousands of Greeks lived and worked in India over the course of more than three centuries, it is only natural that aspects of their language would rub off on the locals. This is indeed what occurred, as a fair number of Greek words permanently entered the major Indian language of Sanskrit. The Sanskrit words for "pen" and "ink" constitute a well-known example. The Greek word for "ink," *melan*, became *mela* in Sanskrit, and the Greek term for "pen," *kalamos*, became *kalamo* in Sanskrit. Similarly, the Greek *puksinon*, meaning "book," became the Sanskrit *pustaka*; *khalinos*, or "horse bridle," became *khalina*; and *barbaros*, or "barbarian," became *barara*.

Ideas from Greek Astronomy

Still another example of Greek influence on Indian society can be found in the scientific disciplines, especially astronomy. Beginning in the 500s BCE, a number of Greek thinkers became the world's first true scientists. They and their successors made major strides in astronomy, including recognizing that the earth is a sphere and fairly accurately calculating the planet's circumference. Other Greeks maintained the age-old premise of astrology (now recognized as a false science)—the idea that the stars and other heavenly bodies affect human lives and fates. Often, popular Greek writers combined concepts from astronomy and astrology in a single book.

Writings of this kind spread throughout much of the ancient world, including India in the centuries following Alexander's conquests. Over time, either Greeks born in India or Indians who had learned to read and write Greek translated Greek books about the heavens into Sanskrit. Perhaps the most influential of these translations was the *Yavanajataka*, or "The Sayings of the Greeks." (*Yavana* was the Indian word for a Greek.) It appeared in 149 or 150 CE in one of the western Indian kingdoms.

The actual Indian name of the *Yavanajataka*'s author is uncertain, but he became known as Yavanesvara, meaning "Lord of the Greeks." The work, which was likely based on a Greek book published earlier in Greek-ruled Egypt, provides general information about the stars and planets. It also tells the reader how to make an astrological chart, or horoscope, based on the time and place of his or her birth.

"The science of astronomy originated with [the Greeks] and for this they must be revered like gods."[28]

—Sixth-century-CE Indian astronomer Varahamihira

Later Greek books that dealt more with the scientific principles of astronomy and mathematics also reached India. The great sixth-century-CE Indian astronomer and mathematician Varahamihira was one of the many Indian scholars influenced by such works. He gave credit, although in a backhanded way, to Greek scientists in his often-cited remark, "The *Yavanas* are barbarians, yet the science of astronomy originated with them and for this they must be revered like gods."[28]

Indo-Greek Artists and the "Man-God"

Particularly important in ancient India were Greek artistic influences, some of which later came to be designated "Greco-Buddhist." They evolved from the painting, sculptural, and architectural styles and ideas that Alexander and his successors brought into northern Bactria and northwestern India, a region the Indians called Gandhara. Between

This statue of the Buddha comes from Gandhara, a region now straddling northeastern Afghanistan and northwestern Pakistan, and dates from the second or third century CE. Showing him physically, as a person with wavy hair, was a Greek artistic innovation.

the late 300s and mid-100s BCE, those artistic traditions took firm root and became widely popular there. Greek rule in the area ended when the Parthians (from northern Iran) invaded in the following century. Yet many Greeks remained in residence there. What is more, the Parthians themselves, along with local Indians, continued to admire and perpetuate Greek artistic traditions.

Early Greek Images of the Buddha

Indo-Greek artists were the first people in history to portray the Buddha, founder of Buddhism, in human form. The earlier tradition in India, where that faith first emerged, was to create artistic versions of objects related to the Buddha, rather than images of his face and body. No one knows for sure if the Indo-Greek artists who began the new practice of making such images employed an actual human prototype, or model. But some scholars suspect they did. The Buddha himself was no longer living, so the model for his statues, if any, would have been someone who lived in the Indo-Greek community.

One theory is that the Greco-Bactrian king Demetrius I (reigned 205–171 BCE) was the prototype for the first statues and drawings of the Buddha. Strengthening that hypothesis is the fact that those images do endow Buddhism's founder with the noble stature of royalty. Whether or not Demetrius actually was the model for such images, over time other Greco-Buddhist artistic elements became associated with likenesses of the Buddha. For a while, for example, many Indian carvings of the Buddha included a second figure standing beside and seemingly protecting him. That figure, who carried a club, was none other than the renowned Greek mythical hero Heracles (known better today as Hercules). This further bolsters the theory that Demetrius posed for the initial statues of the Buddha. Surviving coins minted by that Greek monarch's government show him—and his son—guarded by the figure of the legendary strongman Heracles.

What made these artistic ideas unique was that they combined local Buddhist themes and concepts with Greek ones. Before this hybrid style developed, Indian Buddhist art was aniconic, meaning that it did not picture the Buddha as a person. Instead, by tradition, artists used images of nonliving symbols to represent the founder of Buddhism, who had founded the faith not long before, in the 400s BCE. These objects included the Buddha's favorite tree, his footprints, his prayer wheel, and so forth.

In comparison, traditional Greek art used a markedly different approach to fashioning artistic representations of religious icons. Artists in Greece regularly sculpted realistic statues, figurines, and busts of gods and mythical heroes. The Indo-Greeks inherited that creative practice, and they became the first people to carve statues depicting the Buddha in human form. Most often they showed him with wavy hair. They also dressed him in sandals and a cloak that draped into folds, as well as surrounded him with sculpted decorations, often acanthus leaves. All of these were typical Greek artistic images.

Despite the fact that the Buddha was not a deity, Greek sculptors and other artists initiated the now almost universal portrayal of that religious figure as a sort of "man-god." Indeed, as the faith eventually spread far and wide outside of India, other Asian peoples admired and adopted that approach to depicting the Buddha. In later ages, most Buddhists in China, Korea, Japan, and elsewhere had no inkling that their statues of him were based on original Greek designs. One noted Western art historian points out that the standard Asian image of the Buddha actually resembles a Greek god rather than a more typical Eastern religious figure.

In these and other ways, Alexander's invasion of India in the late fourth century BCE had far-reaching effects on Indian culture that no one could have foreseen at the time. Through decades, which grew into centuries, Greeks and Indians across the Indus Valley intermingled. In the process, Greek linguistic, artistic, and other cultural ideas took firm root, and their effects, though no longer obvious to most people, can still be felt today.

CHAPTER FOUR

How Did Foreign Invasions Give Rise to India's Largest Empire?

Focus Questions

1. Do you believe the invasion of another country can ever be justified? Provide examples to help explain your answer.
2. What qualities do you think matter most for someone who wishes to lead a nation, and why are these qualities important?
3. At what point should a nation's leaders abandon efforts to achieve diplomatic solutions in favor of warfare—and why?

In about 516 BCE, close to two centuries before Alexander's invasion of the Indus Valley, the Persian ruler Darius I invaded that same region and brought part of it into the Persian Empire. Both invasions and the subsequent rule of both the Persians and Greeks in India remained largely confined to its western sector. No serious Persian or Greek penetration of eastern India occurred.

That eastern region, along with the Deccan plateau and areas lying still farther south, were composed of more than a dozen kingdoms of various sizes. All were dominated by the large realm of Magadha, centered in northeastern India. In a very real way, the Persian and Greek invasions of the Indus Valley did the Magadhans a major favor. Thanks to the way those incursions played out, both the foreigners and the western Indian realms stayed out of Magadha's territory and affairs for several centuries. That allowed a series of Magadhan rulers to concentrate their strength and follow their ambitions in the east.

In particular, the Mauryan Empire, centered in Magadha, expanded significantly in both size and power between 322 and 185 BCE.

That realm, John Keay points out, was "the most extensive ever forged by an Indian dynasty."[29] At its height, it stretched from the Indus Valley in the west to the Bay of Bengal in the east and incorporated most of southern India as well.

Among the reasons why the Mauryan state was so successful were that it was wealthy, well-organized, and blessed with many strong rulers and administrators. The late, noted scholar Chester G. Starr called it "an autocratic, centralized realm," and compared it to Ptolemaic (Greek-ruled) Egypt in the same period. In Mauryan Magadha, as in Ptolemaic Egypt, Starr wrote, "irrigation and the distribution of water were carefully regulated, and heavy taxes were exacted for the maintenance of the controllers and inspectors of the bureaucracy and the large professional army. Royal monopolies in metallurgy and mining, based on the copper and iron mines of south Bihar [northern Magadha] furnished further revenues."[30]

Early Magadha and the Persian Incursion

Because solid archaeological and literary evidence remains sketchy, not much is known about Magadha before the Persians invaded western India in the late 500s BCE. What seems fairly certain, however, is by that time it was the richest and militarily strongest of the roughly dozen early Indian kingdoms called the Mahajanapadas. In about 543 BCE, the first strong Magadhan raja, Bimbisara, ascended the local throne. He overran the state of Kashi, situated northwest of central Magadha. He also defeated and absorbed the kingdom of Anga, lying north of the Bay of Bengal.

Bimbisara's son and successor, Ajatashatru (reigned ca. 491–461 BCE), was also an ambitious monarch who pushed Magadha's borders outward. He attacked Kosala, lying northwest of Kashi. According to Keay, he trapped and annihilated the Kosalan army, which was "camped in the dry bed of the river Rapti." After that pivotal event, "although the ancient sources are silent on the details, Ajatashatru seems to have overrun Kosala, which promptly disappears from the record."[31] Ajatashatru also erected a magnificent new capital, Pataliputra, on the northern bank of the Ganges River.

While these conquests were making Magadha stronger in eastern India, a thousand miles to the west the Persians entered and seized

The Persian Empire's third king, Darius I, receives gifts from some of his subjects in one of his many palaces. An aggressive ruler, Darius expanded his realm into India's Indus River valley in the late 500s BCE.

control of sections of the Indus Valley. According to the fifth-century-BCE Greek historian Herodotus, Persia's King Darius I ordered some advance scouts to secretly explore as much of that valley as possible. "He wanted to find out where the Indus joins the sea," Herodotus said of Darius. "And for this purpose [he] sent off on an expedition down the river a number of men whose word he could trust."[32] These explorers, led by an individual named Skylax, managed to find the river's delta, and after a voyage lasting over two years, they returned to Darius's court.

Not long afterward Darius led his army into the Indus Valley. The lands he captured there became the Persian satrapy, or province, of Gandhara (named for the main Indian realm in the area). The wealthiest of Persia's twenty satrapies, it brought large amounts of gold and other valuables into the coffers of Darius and his successors. Moreover, Indian men who dwelled in Gandhara were drafted into the Persian army. Herodotus claimed they were "dressed in cotton [and] carried cane bows and cane arrows tipped with iron." There were also Indian fighters on horseback and "some in chariots drawn by either horses or wild asses."[33]

Mahapadma, His Successors, and Alexander

Fortunately for Magadha's leaders and residents, during this period the Persian kings used their formidable army to attack lands lying far to the west of India (including Greece). Other than an occasional long-range trader, Magadha had no direct contact with the Persians. This allowed Magadhan rulers to channel resources they might have used to defend against Persian attacks into expanding Magadha's army instead. This increasingly large fighting force became a potent tool in Magadhan assaults on other eastern Indian states.

The exploits of the first raja in the third Magadhan dynasty that ruled during the years the Persians occupied the Indus Valley provide a good example. This successful king, Mahapadma Nanda, assumed power sometime between about 424 and the 300s BCE. Mahapadma was an ardent imperialist, or empire builder. Little of a personal nature is known about him. But some evidence suggests that, unlike most or all Indian rajas before and after him, he was born of a family of low social and financial means. Also, it appears that he used ruthless means to gain power. The first-century-CE Roman historian Quintus Curtius Rufus based his account of Mahapadma Nanda on a book by a Greek historian who had interviewed the Indian raja Porus. According to Porus, Curtius reported, Mahapadma's father was a poor "barber whose regular employment barely kept starvation at bay. But by his good looks, he won the heart of the queen. By her, he had been [introduced to] the king of the time, whom he then treacherously murdered, seizing the throne ostensibly as protector of the king's children. He then killed the children."[34]

> "[Indian soldiers] dressed in cotton [and] carried cane bows and cane arrows tipped with iron."[33]
>
> —Fifth-century-BCE Greek historian Herodotus

51

Mahapadma's use of assassination as a political tool seems to have continued in his dealings with other lands. Once in firm control of Magadha, he beefed up the country's already large military forces and invaded a number of neighboring Indian kingdoms. In many cases— quite unlike the way Alexander treated the beaten Porus—Mahapadma proceeded to execute the leaders of the defeated nations. The precise extent of Magadha's growth during the first Nanda raja's reign is uncertain. But it appears to have been substantial. Furthermore, his Nanda successors built on his conquests. During their reigns, Magadha's empire stretched from the Bay of Bengal in the east to the eastern border of the Indus Valley in the west.

These later Nandas (the exact number of whom is debated by historians) managed such expansion in large part because of the quality of their army. It was far bigger and often more battle hardened than the militaries of other Indian states. Indeed, the last Nanda raja, Dhana Nanda, was in charge of the Magadhan realm at the time of Alexander's invasion of western India in the 320s BCE. It was Dhana's huge army that Alexander's soldiers heard rumors about and loathed to encounter. Although the figures for that Magadhan force later quoted by Plutarch (including two hundred thousand infantry and six thousand elephants) were surely exaggerated, Dhana's army was likely two to three times larger than Alexander's.

Rise of Chandragupta and Kautilya

The fact that Alexander and his forces did turn back and thereby failed to engage with Magadha's army was a tremendous gift to that Indian country and its imperial realm. Alexander was unarguably a gifted military leader, and his soldiers were among the best, if not *the* best, in the world. He and his men had already defeated armies larger than their own on several occasions. Modern experts agree, therefore, that at the very least they would have inflicted heavy losses on the Magadhan forces. But because no such losses occurred, in the years that followed, Magadha maintained its army at full strength and therefore had little to fear from its Indian enemies.

One of the Indian rulers who benefited significantly from this boon was the one who ended the Nanda dynasty and started one of his own. Despite the Nandas' large, efficient military, in their domestic af-

A painting depicts the Magadhan ruler Chandragupta Maurya (right), conversing with his chief adviser, a teacher-turned-statesman named Kautilya. Chandragupta founded the hugely successful Mauryan dynasty.

fairs they were often inept and/or corrupt, which made them very unpopular with their subjects. This created a setting that was ripe for an ambitious and skilled leader to depose the regime and take the throne.

Indeed, that very scenario played out in about 322 BCE. An individual named Chandragupta Maurya, closely aided by a holy man—a Brahmin named Kautilya—led two rebellions against the Nandas. The second revolt was a major success. "The last Nanda was sent packing, quite literally," Keay writes. "He is supposed to have been spared

Ancient Indian Soldiers' Weapons

Much has been made by both ancient and modern writers about the size and effectiveness of the Magadhan army commanded by Nandan and Mauryan rulers. Not much is known for sure about the weapons, armor, and tactics of the soldiers of that army. Somewhat helpful in that respect is this excerpt from the *Indica*, a short book penned by Alexander the Great's ancient biographer Arrian. (Arrian took a fair amount of his information from a book of the same name by another ancient Greek, Megasthenes, who had spent time at the Mauryan royal court.) This excerpt describes the weapons wielded by typical Indian warriors during Alexander's era.

> The infantry [foot soldiers] have a bow, of the height of the owner. This they poise on the ground, and set their left foot against it, and shoot thus; drawing the bowstring a very long way back. [Nothing] can stand against an arrow shot by an Indian archer, neither shield nor breast-plate nor any strong armor. In their left hands they carry small shields of untanned hide. [Some soldiers] have javelins in place of bows. All carry a broad scimitar [sword with a curved blade], [used] when they have a hand-to-hand fight. [Their] horsemen have two javelins, like lances, and a small shield smaller than the infantry's. The horses have no saddles, nor do they use Greek bits nor any like the Celtic bits, but round the end of the horses' mouths they have an untanned stitched rein fitted.

Arrian, *Indica*, trans. E.I. Robson, Ancient History Sourcebook, Fordham University, 2000. http://sourcebooks.fordham.edu.

only his life, plus [any] of his legendary wealth as he could crate and carry away, [and] Chandragupta Maurya ascended the Magadhan throne."[35]

The new raja appears to have been only around twenty-five when he assumed power. Although he had no prior experience in politics, he quickly proved that he possessed considerable natural abilities as a leader. It is difficult to tell so long after the fact, but at least part of his effectiveness as Magadha's king was likely the result of the advice he received from Kautilya, who remained always at his side as his chief adviser.

In fact, later Indians came to view Kautilya as a statesman of the first order. He was credited with writing a long work, which survives intact, titled the *Arthashastra* (translating literally as "Science of Material Gain"). "It can be thought of as an encyclopedia of information on the ancient Indian world," Indian writer Sumedha Ojha explains. Its sub-

> "The last Nanda was sent packing, quite literally."[35]
>
> —Historian John Keay

jects range "from kings to spies and ministers, from cotton to spices and pearls, from inheritance to divorce and municipal law, foreign relations to forts and cities, magic incantations to justice and political administration." Ojha describes the topics of only four of the *Arthashastra*'s fifteen sections, or "books," saying:

> The first book deals with the training and equipment of the king as a ruler; and being a "Kautilyan King" is no mean task. He cannot sleep for more than four hours a day and has a full and punishing routine for the rest of the twenty hours. Book Two deals with the activities of the state in various fields. Thirty-four departments are described with activities ranging around the fields of agriculture, forestry, cattle, horses, elephants, yarns, liquor, army, issue of passports, trade, customs, shipping, etc. Book Three sets down a code of law, the fourth [book] deals with the suppression of crime.[36]

Leader and Conquerer

Evidence suggests that Chandragupta lived up to the ideal of being a "Kautilyan King." A Greek historian named Megasthenes, who spent considerable time at the Mauryan court, called him a tireless, highly dedicated ruler. His many military successes were no doubt due in part to the large size and high quality of the Magadhan army. But one must also factor in the debt that Chandragupta owed Alexander the Great, who died only a year before the younger man ascended Magadha's throne. In the words of historian Vincent A. Smith, "It is certain that the troubles [among Greek leaders] consequent upon the death of Alexander in the summer of 323 BCE gave young Chandragupta his opportunity." He struck out at several of his nearby Indian neighbors and even attacked some towns in the eastern Indus Valley. "When all opposition had been crushed," Smith continues, "Chandragupta, in the vigor of his early manhood, stood forth as the unquestioned master of northern India."[37]

While campaigning in the Indus Valley sometime after 311 BCE, Chandragupta and his soldiers came face-to-face with Greek forces who were guarding some of the towns that Alexander had overrun not long before. These Greeks owed their allegiance to Seleucus, one of Alexander's chief lieutenants. By this time Seleucus had gained control of what are now Iraq and Iran, along with most of Bactria and sections of western India.

> "Chandragupta, in the vigor of his early manhood, stood forth as the unquestioned master of northern India."[37]
>
> —Scholar Vincent A. Smith

At first the Magadhan and Seleucid forces engaged in some skirmishes. But soon both sides saw the wisdom of making peace. Seleucus did not wish to waste troops and material resources fighting an uphill battle against the enormous Magadhan army. As for Chandragupta, he was well aware of how much he had gained by not having to fight Alexander's army. Now the powerful Indian ruler applied the same reasoning to his dealings with Seleucus, whose forces were formidable in their own right.

A formal treaty between the Mauryan and Seleucid empires was signed in about 305 BCE, around eighteen years after Alexander's untimely passing. Seleucus yielded several Greek-controlled territories west of the Indus to Chandragupta. In return, the latter gave his new ally five hundred battle elephants. Also, it appears that the Magadhan raja gave his young daughter in marriage to one of Seleucus's sons (although some experts think it was the opposite—that a Mauryan prince married a Greek princess).

A surviving bust shows Seleucus I, founder of the Seleucid Empire, one of the three largest kingdoms created by Alexander's so-called successors (*Diadochoi* in Greek). Alexander, Seleucus, and other Greek rulers introduced Greek culture into western India.

No One Exists in Isolation

In these ways Chandragupta Maurya came to control more of India than any ruler before him. He may well have expanded his huge empire even farther, perhaps both within and south of the Deccan, where a few lands still remained independent. In 301 BCE, however, at the height of his power, the Magadhan king did something totally unexpected and unprecedented. He abdicated his throne, leaving it to his son Bindusara, and became a monk dedicated to a life of poverty.

Kautilya's *Arthashastra* contains a great deal of general information about Indian society and traditions during the late fourth century BCE. The statements quoted here are part of the section describing customs relating to divorce and adultery.

A woman who hates her husband, who has passed the period of seven turns of her menses [monthly period], and who loves another [man], shall immediately return to her husband both the endowment and jewelry she has received from him, and allow him to lie down with another woman. A man, hating his wife, shall allow her to take shelter in the house of a beggar woman, or of her lawful guardians or of her kinsmen. . . . A woman, hating her husband, cannot divorce her husband against his will. Nor can a man divorce his wife against her will. But from mutual enmity divorce may be obtained. . . . If a woman goes out while the husband is asleep or intoxicated, or if she shuts the door of the house against her husband, she shall be fined twelve panas. If a woman keeps him out of the house at night, she shall pay double the above fine. If a man and a woman make signs to each other with a view to sensual enjoyment, or carry on secret conversation for the same purpose, the woman shall pay a fine of twenty-four panas and the man double that amount.

Kautilya, *Arthashastra*, trans. R. Shamasasty, Indian History Sourcebook, Fordham University, 1998. http://sourcebooks.fordham.edu.

(He professed the Jain religion, established in India more than two centuries before.) Then the former raja starved himself to death. This was the official scenario put out by the Magadhan government. Some modern scholars think it may have been a cover story for a nefarious murder plot. They point out that suddenly giving up power the way Chandragupta supposedly did was very out of character for him. It is possible, they say, that Bindusara had his father killed and then made up the abdication and self-starvation story to divert attention from the crime.

No matter how Bindusara actually acquired the Magadhan throne, he ruled until about 269 BCE, some thirty-two years in all. Like his father, he had military ambitions and managed to expand the realm by capturing several sections of the Deccan. When Bindusara died, the Mauryan Empire, centered in Magadha, was far larger than any native Indian nation or kingdom had ever been. Moreover, to a substantial degree that outcome had been made possible by a series of events set in motion by the Persian and Greek invasions in the prior two and a half centuries. As in all times and places in history, no people, nation, or empire exists in isolation. Rather, all are at times shaped in unanticipated ways by unforeseen events that can and occasionally do originate in distant lands.

CHAPTER FIVE

How Did One Indian Ruler Help Transform Buddhism into a World Religion?

Focus Questions

1. Do you think humans are capable of living in a world without war? Why or why not?
2. In what ways does Buddhism seem similar to and different from other major religions?
3. How would you define religious tolerance, and how might it benefit or impede a society? Provide examples to help explain your answer.

Chandragupta Maurya and his immediate successors significantly expanded the empire centered in the ancient kingdom of Magadha, making it the largest imperial realm in Indian history. At the time this appeared to be a feat of tremendous proportions, and in some ways it was. Yet as it turned out, this was not the Mauryan dynasty's greatest and longest-lasting achievement. No one then alive could foresee that a later Mauryan ruler would generate a far larger expansion, although of a markedly different kind.

The raja in question was Chandragupta's grandson—Ashoka. Like his grandfather—and father, Bindusara, as well—Ashoka began his reign by immersing himself in military culture and leading the imperial army in conquests. But though successful, these endeavors pale in comparison to Ashoka's most outstanding accomplishment. More than any other single individual, he was responsible for making Buddhism a world religion. He did not only adopt that faith himself. He also sent out missionaries, an effort that in time transformed Buddhism from a small-scale, local faith into a major, international one.

"Herein lies the greatness of Ashoka," historian R.K. Mookerji writes. "No victorious monarch in the history of the world is known to have ever [achieved] anything like it."[38]

Ashoka the Conqueror

Exactly how Ashoka, whose name means "the sorrowless one," managed to acquire Magadha's throne remains somewhat of a mystery. His father died in about 269 BCE, but Ashoka did not emerge as king until a few years later. Most modern experts think that when the father died, a power struggle erupted among several of his sons. The names of most of those princes, as well as the parts they played in the fight for the throne, have been lost to history. The only certain fact relating to these royal intrigues is that sometime in the mid-260s BCE Ashoka won out over his siblings and became raja.

> "No victorious monarch in the history of the world is known to have ever [achieved] anything like it."[38]
>
> —Historian R.K. Mookerji

Evidence suggests that Ashoka's initial priority as Magadha's leader was to carry on the militaristic legacy of former members of the Mauryan royal family. At the time he ascended the throne, there was only one major nation-state in northern India that was not yet a part of the Mauryan Empire. The kingdom in question was Kalinga, situated in India's east-central sector, bordering the Bay of Bengal.

The precise date when Ashoka launched a full-scale invasion of Kalinga is uncertain, but it appears that his victory was complete by about 260 BCE. That victory was overwhelming, as the Kalingans had little or no chance of repelling the huge Magadhan army. Ashoka's own public records stated that one hundred thousand Kalingans were slain and another one hundred and fifty thousand were left homeless. Many thousands more died of wounds, illness, or hunger in the months that followed.

Most modern scholars think these figures may have been overstated. But even if that is the case, the slaughter and subsequent misery in Kalinga must have been considerable. Later generations of Indians looked back on the incident as a terrible stain on their history. Perhaps more significantly, the carnage in Kalinga brought about a crucial change in the thinking of the very man who had instigated it.

A carving depicts King Ashoka on his chariot and accompanied by some of his soldiers. After conquering the neighboring kingdom of Kalinga, he had an unprecedented change of heart and renounced the concept of military aggression.

A Major Change of Heart

Indeed, after touring Kalinga after the war and surveying the damage his army had inflicted, Ashoka claimed to be shocked and saddened. It is unknown why he had been naïve enough to later be so stunned and shaken by the grim realities of full-scale war. Perhaps, like so many inexperienced, idealistic young men, he had pictured battle in a romanticized way—as a colorful contest among gallant, heroic warriors.

Whatever Ashoka's unrealistic youthful visions of war had been, the harsh realities of the human suffering he and his soldiers had caused hit him hard. As a result, he suddenly underwent a major change of heart. Moreover, he was not the stereotypical craven politician who tries to deny and evade responsibility for his mistakes. Rather, he possessed the courage and decency to publicly admit he had done something he viewed as wrong.

In those days, of course, no electronic or other forms of modern-style media existed. So Ashoka had only two choices at his disposal to address his subjects, and he employed both of them. One was to have special messengers stand in local town squares and recite aloud a text the raja had prepared. The other approach was to have sculptors inscribe, or carve, that same text onto stone panels and pillars and large, prominent rocks throughout his realm. Hence, they became known as the "Rock Edicts" and "Pillar Edicts." Among the several of these carved statements that have survived, one reads in part:

[I] feel deep remorse for having conquered the Kalingans. [I am] deeply pained by the killing, dying, and deportation that take place when an unconquered country is conquered. But [I am] pained even more [when that country's people] are injured, killed or separated from their loved ones. Even those who are not affected by all this suffer when they see friends, acquaintances, companions and relatives affected. These misfortunes befall all as a result of war, and this pains [me]. Therefore the killing, death, or deportation of a hundredth, or even a thousandth part of those who died during the conquest of Kalinga now pains [me]. Truly, [I believe it would be more moral to promote] non-injury, restraint, and impartiality to all beings.[39]

The point Ashoka made about morality is key to what happened next. Clearly, he realized that simply apologizing for what he had done was not enough and constituted only a first step in creating a new national policy relating to war. He recognized that a necessary second step would be to make his actions speak louder than his words. So he took the major step of converting to Buddhism.

Advocating Certain Buddhist Concepts

At the time, a majority of Indians were Hindus, not Buddhists. At first glance, therefore, it may seem strange that the king chose to become a member of what was then a minority faith among his many subjects. This move was well calculated, however. Ashoka, who had been a Hindu since childhood, knew that Hinduism had many fine qualities as a religion. But its teachings, though far from militant, allowed for committing violent acts under certain circumstances, notably in defending the faithful from attack. In contrast, Ashoka knew, Buddhism advocated respect for all living things and nonviolent behavior in *all* situations. Thus, in choosing to become a Buddhist, Ashoka made the powerful statement that violence against any and all peoples and nations was wrong.

Ashoka evidently also used his expression of remorse and conversion to Buddhism as a sort of teaching moment for his subjects. First, he made the point in his Rock Edicts that all faiths were worthy and that none should be rejected or persecuted. Also, Buddhists were encouraged to explain their beliefs to their non-Buddhist neighbors. Those individuals learned that, like early Hindus, early Buddhists recognized the existence of various special, or divine, beings. An important difference was that Hindus saw these beings as powerful gods who controlled the heavens and the earth; whereas Buddhists believed those beings were not all-powerful. Instead, they, along with humans, were subject to the universe's inherent laws. Also, Buddhists recognized their beliefs less as a formal religion and more as a philosophy, or manner of viewing life and humanity's place in the universal scheme. For them, Buddhism was a kind of path to finding knowledge and peace with oneself, one's community, and the greater universe. A Buddhist could discover that path with the aid of priests. Or he or she could try to achieve that goal on his or her own.

Most non-Buddhists in Ashoka's imperial domains already knew that Buddhism had been built on the life and teachings of a man known as "the Buddha." A somewhat mysterious figure, supposedly he had been born Siddhartha Gautama, a prince of a northern Indian kingdom, about three centuries before Ashoka's time. It was said that Siddhartha's childhood had been happy and carefree. But when he was in his twenties, he had learned for the first time of the existence of human suffering.

Siddhartha was so shocked and dismayed by this discovery, the story went, that he decided to give up his comfortable life in his father's palace. He now devoted himself to seclusion and meditation, as Hindu monks did. Adopting extreme self-discipline and self-denial, he sought

Between 399 and 412 CE, a Chinese traveler named Fa-Hsien paid a visit to India. A committed Buddhist, thanks to the missionaries Ashoka had sent to China centuries before, he sought to feel closer to the Buddha by touring some of the sites that the noted religious leader had once frequented. In the travel guide Fa-Hsien later penned, he recalled visiting a hill where, it was believed, the Buddha had once walked and chanted. Beneath the steep cliffs on "the north of the mountain," Fa-Hsien wrote, the Buddha's follower Devadatta had tossed a rock that had accidentally

> hurt Buddha's toes. The rock is still there. The hall where Buddha preached his [beliefs] has been destroyed, and only the foundations of the brick walls remain. On this hill the peak is beautifully green, and rises grandly up; it is the highest of all the five hills [in the area]. I bought incense, flowers, oil, and lamps, and hired two [local men] to carry them to the peak. When I got to it, I made offerings with the flowers and incense, and lighted the lamps when the darkness began to come on. I felt melancholy, but restrained my tears and said, "Here the Buddha [preached]. I, Fa-hsien, was born when I could not meet with the Buddha; and now I only see the footprints which he has left, and the place where he lived, and nothing more."

Fa-Hsien, *Record of Buddhistic Kingdoms*, trans. James Legge, Project Gutenberg, 2013. www.gutenberg.org.

to understand the causes of human suffering and find some way to alleviate it. Hopefully, that would allow him to attain true wisdom.

As Ashoka himself told his subjects, one day the young prince-turned-monk had a sudden realization. He achieved a vision of the meaning of human existence and thereby became the Buddha, or "Enlightened One." Not only did he see what caused human

This painting on a temple wall is part of Korean Buddhism. As the faith spread outward from India, various east Asian peoples adopted its principles, among them the Chinese, Japanese, and Koreans. The image features the Buddha attended by his earliest followers.

suffering—arrogance and greed—he also realized how such suffering can be overcome. The key, he said, was to implement a simple code of everyday conduct that he called the Eightfold Path. Much of it involved being kind, honest, and generous.

The Buddha began traveling around India, Ashoka recalled. As the philosopher-prophet visited village after village, he preached his beliefs about recognizing the causes of suffering and learning how to overcome it. After his death, his followers continued spreading these ideas. Hearing them, a few Hindus converted to Buddhism. Far more Hindus instead tried to reconcile the Buddhist concepts of right living with existing Hindu principles. In this way, many Hindu Indians accepted certain Buddhist concepts without giving up all their traditional beliefs.

Embracing Dharma

One particular Buddhist concept that Ashoka promoted above most others was that of dharma, which translates approximately as "moral conquest" or "moral law." The raja himself tried to define it for his

The Buddha's Steps to Achieving Happiness

When Ashoka converted to Buddhism, he took to heart the discoveries that the Buddha had made in the process of becoming enlightened. After much soul searching and meditation, the former Siddhartha concluded that four basic truths define human existence. The first is that life is filled with suffering, and the second identifies the causes of that suffering as excessive pride, greed, and self-indulgence. The third basic truth is that those failings are not unavoidable and that people can learn to overcome them. The most profound of the four great truths, according to the Buddha, is the means of overcoming human suffering's causes. It consists of a series of positive actions or steps that he called the Eightfold Path. The first step is right views, or understanding; the second is having the right goals; then comes right speech; followed by right behavior; choosing the right job, or type of livelihood; making an honest effort to do right; right thoughts, or awareness of life's realities; and applying the proper amount of concentration, or meditation. In addition to conforming to this eight-part path of proper steps and behaviors, the Buddha said, people should refrain from killing living things. They should also refrain from stealing, telling falsehoods, getting drunk, and indulging in sex outside of marriage. If a person followed all these steps, Buddhism's founder stated, he or she could achieve a true state of peace and happiness.

subjects in some of the texts he made public in his Rock Edicts. Dharma, he explained, is a person's attempt to strive for "goodness, kindness, generosity, truthfulness, and purity." While embracing these ideals, he said, people should try to steer clear of "cruelty, anger, pride, jealousy," and especially violence. By using this approach to daily living, Ashoka insisted, one would have a good chance of finding "happiness in this world and the next."[40]

According to Ashoka, dharma also held that slaughtering various animals for their meat and hides was unethical. So he passed new laws that protected geese, ducks, parrots, pigeons, and other kinds of birds that had been regularly hunted in the past, as well as bats, tortoises, porcupines, deer, cattle, squirrels, and wild asses. One Pillar Edict declared, "Those nanny goats, ewes, and sows which are with young or giving milk to their young are protected, and so are young ones less than six months old." Moreover, "forests are not to be burnt [in order] to kill creatures."[41] As a result of these new laws, meat eating significantly declined in India.

Still another quality of dharma, Ashoka explained, was the importance it placed on respect for people of all walks of life, no matter what their social station might be. Employers and their employees, teachers and their students, neighbors and monks all must be treated with dignity. Further, proper treatment of others was a type of ceremony, or social ritual. The text of one of his Rock Edicts said in part:

> A father, a son, a brother, a master, a friend, a companion, and even a neighbor should say: "This is good, this is the ceremony that should be performed until its purpose is fulfilled, [so] this I shall do." [The] ceremony of Dharma is timeless. Even if it does not achieve its purpose in this world, it produces great merit in the next, whereas if it does achieve its purpose in this world, one gets great merit both here and there.[42]

Erecting Buddhist Temples

Ashoka's conversion to and support for Buddhism did much to promote that still fairly young faith. But because Hinduism was far more established in India, Buddhism spread somewhat slowly within the Mauryan Empire.

Considerably more striking was the measurable effect that early Buddhism had on ancient Indian architecture. Like nearly all ancient peoples, the Indians were devoutly religious. So they sank a great deal of time and money into building temples dedicated to their gods. The first formal Indian religious temples, which appeared in the early first millennium BCE, were based on an architectural form called the stupa. Initially, it consisted of a circular earthen burial mound. As time went on, however, these mounds became dome-shaped structures composed of stone blocks and/or fired bricks, all of which were carefully and colorfully painted. Some of the more advanced stupas became quite large and complex.

The initial Indian stupas were erected by Hindu worshippers. But after Buddhism emerged in India in the 400s BCE, Buddhists began building those circular structures too. (They were not designed for worshipping the Buddha, since he was a human being rather than a god. Instead, Buddhist stupas were places where the faithful could gather and meditate together.) One of the finest surviving examples of those Buddhist meeting places is the Great Stupa at Sanchi, in north-central

The Great Stupa at Sanchi remains in excellent condition. The structure was begun by the Indian ruler Ashoka in the third century BCE. Many of its splendid sculptures depict episodes from the Buddha's life.

India. An impressive edifice, it stands 120 feet (37 m) across and 54 feet (16.5 m) tall. Modern experts think that Ashoka erected it, along with several other stupa-style temples, as part of his pro-Buddhist policy.

Inside India and Beyond

An even more important aspect of Ashoka's contribution to the rise of Buddhism was his role in spreading that faith far beyond India's borders. Before he became raja of Magadha and leader of the Mauryan realm, clusters of Buddhists existed mainly in sections of the upper Ganges River valley, directly south of the vast Himalayan mountain chain. Ashoka first sought to expand Buddhism within India itself. His opening move was to make that faith the official imperial religion. This was meant only to create a royal example that he hoped at least some others might follow. Hindus, Jains, and members of other faiths were not required to convert to Buddhism.

Indeed, Ashoka strongly emphasized the importance of religious toleration, saying that all faiths were worthy of respect. In one of his carved edicts, he advocated:

> It is better to honor other religions. By so doing, one's own religion benefits, and so do other religions, while doing otherwise harms one's own religion and the religions of others. Whoever praises his own religion, due to excessive devotion, and condemns others with the thought "Let me glorify my own religion," only harms his own religion. Therefore contact between religions is good. One should listen to and respect the doctrines professed by others.[43]

Moreover, despite Ashoka's own conversion to Buddhism, he did not actually preach that faith's precepts to his people in an attempt to convert them. Rather, in his famous edicts he promoted universal concepts advocated by all religions—such as peace, justice, social harmony, and compassion. He ordered some of his officials to devote their energies to aiding poor and sick people, protected many animals from slaughter, and urged people to be honest, kind, and generous with one another.

As for Ashoka's promotion of Buddhism beyond India's borders, he sent out well-trained missionaries to many foreign lands. They included Cambodia, Thailand, Korea, China, and Japan, among others. At first, only a few residents of these regions fully converted to Buddhism. Some others, as a number of Indian Hindus had, accepted certain Buddhist concepts and worked them into their existing religious systems.

Over time, however, more and more people in those foreign lands converted completely to Buddhism. In some cases the leaders of a nation converted first and subsequently used their considerable influence to convince others to join the faith. A notable example of this scenario took place in Ceylon—today called Sri Lanka—the island nation lying off India's southeastern coast. Some ancient sources claim that Ashoka called forth his son, Mahinda, and his daughter, Sanghamitta, who had recently become Buddhists themselves.

> "It is better to honor other religions. By so doing, one's own religion benefits."[43]
>
> —The ancient Indian raja Ashoka

He asked them to travel to Ceylon and describe Buddhist principles to that nation's ruler, King Tissa. In fairly short order, Tissa and the members of his royal court converted, and then Tissa introduced Buddhism to his people. They steadily adopted the religion, which had formerly existed only in India, and thereafter Buddhism was Sri Lanka's primary faith. It remains so today.

Ashoka's Impact

In fact, thanks in part to Ashoka's efforts, today Buddhism is practiced all over the world, particularly in Asia. By 2016 more than 500 million people—making up about 7 percent of the global population—identified themselves as Buddhists. "Ashoka's influence had a major impact on Buddhism," says Barbara O'Brien, an American expert on that religion. "Before Ashoka, the Buddha's teachings could be found only in a portion of present-day India." After Ashoka's diligent efforts to promote that faith, she points out, it "was known far beyond India."[44]

University of Maryland professor Cathy Gorn is one of several scholars who give even more weight to that ancient leader's accomplishment. "Without the missionary directive of King Ashoka," she states, "Buddhism as a religion might not exist."[45]

Introduction: India's Amazing Cultural Preservation

1. Quoted in Mukhtan Ahmed, *Ancient Pakistan: An Archaeological Survey*. New York: Amazon Digital Services, 2014, p. 48.
2. Charles Gates, *Ancient Cities: The Archaeology of Urban Life in the Ancient Near East and Egypt, Greece, and Rome*. London: Routledge, 2007, p. 71.
3. Bridget Allchin and Raymond Allchin, *The Rise of Civilization in India and Pakistan*. Cambridge: Cambridge University Press, 1982, p. 171.
4. Sinharaja Tammita-Delgoda, *A Traveller's History of India*. New York: Interlink, 2003, p. 1.
5. Alain Daniélou, *A Brief History of India*. Rochester, VT: Inner Traditions, 2003, p. v.
6. Tammita-Delgoda, *A Traveller's History of India*, p. 1.

Chapter One: A Brief History of Ancient India

7. Tammita-Delgoda, *A Traveller's History of India*, p. 14.
8. Gordon Johnson, *Cultural Atlas of India*. New York: Facts On File, 1996, p. 62.
9. Herodotus, *The Histories*, trans. Aubrey de Sélincourt. New York: Penguin, 2003, p. 285.
10. Arrian, *Anabasis Alexandri*, published as *The Campaigns of Alexander*, trans. Aubrey de Sélincourt. New York: Penguin, 1986, p. 281.
11. Megasthenes, *Indika*, in *Ancient India Described by Megasthenes and Arrian*, trans. J.W. McCrindle. London: Trubner, 1877, p. 72.
12. Quoted in Ven S. Dhammika, trans., "The Edicts of King Ashoka," Colorado State University, 1994. www.cs.colostate.edu.
13. John Keay, *India: A History*. New York: Grove, 2000, p. 100.
14. Fa-Hsien, *Record of Buddhistic Kingdoms*, trans. James Legge, Project Gutenberg, 2013. www.gutenberg.org.
15. Fa-Hsien, *Record of Buddhistic Kingdoms*.

Chapter Two: What Part Did India's Early Cultures Play in the Birth of Hinduism?

16. Bhagavad-Gita, trans. Barbara S. Miller, PDF Archive, 2014. www.pdf-archive.com.

17. Tammita-Delgoda, *A Traveller's History of India*, p. 48.

18. Peter Britton, "The First Great Chapter in the History of Ancient India Was the Indus Valley Civilization," TimeMaps, 2016. www .timemaps.com.

19. Britton, "The First Great Chapter in the History of Ancient India Was the Indus Valley Civilization."

20. Cristian Violatti, "The Vedas," *Ancient History Encyclopedia*, January 18, 2013. www.ancient.eu.

21. Violatti, "The Vedas."

22. Mortimer Wheeler, *The Indus Civilization*. London: Cambridge University Press, 1968, p. 110.

Chapter Three: How Did Alexander's Invasion of India Alter Indian Culture?

23. Sanujit, "Cultural Links Between India and the Greco-Roman World," *Ancient History Encyclopedia*, February 12, 2011. www .ancient.eu.

24. Keay, *India*, p. 71.

25. Arrian, *Anabasis Alexandri*, pp. 279–80.

26. Plutarch, *Life of Alexander*, in *The Age of Alexander: Nine Greek Lives by Plutarch*, trans. Ian Scott-Kilvert. New York: Penguin, 1993, p. 319.

27. Sanujit, "Cultural Links Between India and the Greco-Roman World."

28. Quoted in H.G. Rawlinson, *Intercourse Between India and the Western World*. New Delhi: Asian Educational Services, 2001, p. 173.

Chapter Four: How Did Foreign Invasions Give Rise to India's Largest Empire?

29. Keay, *India*, p. 83.

30. Chester G. Starr, *A History of the Ancient World*. New York: Oxford University Press, 1991, p. 632.

31. Keay, *India*, p. 67.

32. Herodotus, *The Histories*, pp. 284–85.

33. Herodotus, *The Histories*, pp. 467, 471.

34. Quintus Curtius Rufus, *History of Alexander*, trans. John Yardley. New York: Penguin, 1984, p. 215.

35. Keay, *India*, p. 83.

36. Sumedha Ojha, "How Kautilya's *Arthashastra* Shaped the Telling of Ancient Indian History," *Swarajya*, August 19, 2016. http://swarajyamag.com.

37. Vincent A. Smith, *The Early History of India*. New York: Atlantic, 1999, pp. 43–44.

Chapter Five: How Did One Indian Ruler Help Transform Buddhism into a World Religion?

38. R.K. Mookerji, "Ashoka the Great," in *The History and Culture of the Indian People*, vol. 2, ed. R.C. Majumdar et al. New York: Bharatiya Vidya Bhavan, 2001, p. 74.

39. Quoted in Dhammika, "The Edicts of King Ashoka."

40. Quoted in Dhammika, "The Edicts of King Ashoka."

41. Quoted in Dhammika, "The Edicts of King Ashoka."

42. Quoted in Dhammika, "The Edicts of King Ashoka."

43. Quoted in Dhammika, "The Edicts of King Ashoka."

44. Barbara O'Brien, "The Emperor Ashoka: Patron of Buddhism," About Religion & Spirituality, 2016. http://buddhism.about.com.

45. Quoted in 100 Leaders in World History, "Facts About Ashoka." http://100leaders.org/ashoka.

Books

A.L. Basham, *The Wonder That Was India*. New York: Picador, 2014.

Julian Bound, *Religions of India*. Toronto: SOL, 2016.

John Keay, *India: A History*. New York: Grove, 2011.

Stephen Knapp, *Mysteries of the Ancient Vedic Empire: Recognizing Vedic Contributions to Other Cultures Around the World*. Charleston, SC: Amazon Digital Services, 2015.

Vincent A. Smith, *The Early History of India from 600 B.C. to the Muslim Conquest*. Charleston, SC: Amazon Digital Services, 2014.

Sinharaja Tammita-Delgoda, *A Traveller's History of India*. New York: Interlink, 2011.

Internet Sources

Joseph Berrigan, "Battle of Hydaspes," Ancient Mesopotamia. http://joseph_berrigan.tripod.com/ancientbabylon/id36.html.

K. Krist Hirst, "Mohenjo-Daro: Indus Civilization Capital City in Pakistan," About Education, September 13, 2016. http://archaeology.about.com/od/mterms/qt/mohenjo_daro.htm.

Library of Congress Country Studies, "India: Harappan Culture," About Education, 2016. http://ancienthistory.about.com/od/indusvalleyciv/a/harappanculture.htm.

Joshua J. Mark, "Ancient India," *Ancient History Encyclopedia*, November 13, 2012. www.ancient.eu/india.

Websites

Ancient India, British Museum (www.ancientindia.co.uk). This is the gateway to the British Museum's excellent brief overview of ancient Indian civilization.

Buddhism, BBC (www.bbc.co.uk/religion/religions/Buddhism). This worthwhile website offers links to numerous online essays about this important faith, which originated in ancient India.

History of Hinduism, BBC (www.bbc.co.uk/religion/religions/hinduism/history/history_1.shtml). A superior, detailed overview of the historical roots, phases, and beliefs of Hinduism, one of the world's great religions.